Reunion with the Beloved

Poetry and Martyrdom

Reunion with the Beloved

Poetry and Martyrdom

Translated and Edited by

John S. Hatcher

and

Amrollah Hemmat

JUXTA PUBLISHING LIMITED • HONG KONG

Copyright 2004, John S. Hatcher and Amrollah Hemmat.
All Rights Reserved.

First Edition, June 2004.

Published by Juxta Publishing Ltd. (Hong Kong).
www.juxta.com

Printed in Canada.

Cover design by David Dayco.
www.epiphanygraphics.ca

Illustrations by Jill Hatcher Campisciano

ISBN 988-97451-1-9

All praise to the omnipotent Lord, that in this auspicious day He Who is the Sun of bounty has shone out so fair and bright as to light up the world of the hearts. He has burned away the veils of waywardness and ignorance. He has struck off the fetters of baseless myths and ignoble concepts that chained the people hand and foot. He has cleansed and burnished the mirrors of men's souls, sullied by the dust and rust of this dark world. He has opened wide the door to that Celestial Tavern[1] of matchless wine, and He is freely pouring out the immortal draught of knowledge and perception and love.[2]

Bahíyyih Khánum (The Greatest Holy Leaf)

Dedicated to those
who have sacrificed
affection for water and clay
in the path of the Beloved

Acknowledgements

We would like to express our gratitude to Mrs. Parvin Joneidi, Mr. Muhammad Ebrahim, and Mr. Ehsanollah Hemmat for carefully reviewing some of the poems in this collection in the original language and advising us on alternative interpretations; and to Dr. Kavian Milani for sharing valuable resources with us.

We also would like to thank our colleagues at Payam-i-Doust (Bahá'í International Radio Services) and in particular Ms. Shahnaz Ghassemi.

Last, but not least, we are indebted to Jill Hatcher Campisciano for the artistic renderings of the portraits of Rúhu'lláh and Muná.

Contents

Foreword 15
Preface 21
What is Martyrdom? 21
The Muslim Rationale 23
The Poems as Art 29
The Structure of the Volume 31
Some Cultural Insights 35

Part I: Kings Among Kings 39
Background 39
The Battle at Fort Shaykh Tabarsí 39
Those Who Quaffed the Cup of Martyrdom at Fort Shaykh Tabarsí 43
(1) God is Calling You From this World *by Na'ím* 56
(2) From Varqá with Love *by Varqá (martyred)* 57
(3) From the Mathnaví Anvaríyyih *by Varqá (martyred)* 61
(4) The Lover's Ablution *by Varqá (martyred)* 63
(5) The Garden of Love *by 'Ustád Muhammad 'Alí Salmání* 65
(6) Mazi Dárad *by Liqá'í Káshání* 67
(7) He is the Intended One *by Rúhu'lláh (martyred)* 69
(8) Tears of the Dove *by 'Abdí* 73
(9) Alas! Alas! *by Nayyir and Síná* 79
(10) The Story of Hájí Mullá Hasan *by Nabíl-i-A'zam (martyred)* 82
(11) The Master Builder *by Na'ím* 84
(12) Except in this Faith *by Na'ím* 85
(13) The Unseen Threads of Destiny *by Muhammad Báhau'd-Dín 'Abdí* ... 87
(14) Beyond Heroic Legends: On the Anniversary of the
     Martyrdom of the Báb *by 'Abdí* 88
(15) A Poem of Unity *by Na'ím* 92
(16) 'Abdu'l-Bahá in America (1912) *by Na'ím* 93

Part II: O You Who Claim to Believe 95
Background 95
"The Bahá'í Question" 95
Bahá'ís Executed Since the Revolution 98
(17) Do Not Lay Waste Our Home Again! *by 'Abdí* 106
(18) O Ye That Are Foolish, Yet Have a Name to be Wise *by 'Abdí* 107
(19) Seize the Sure Handle *by Dr. Valíyu'llá Kamál Ábádí* 108
(20) Questions of the Heart *by 'Abdí* 110
(21) The Tavern of Love *by 'Abdí* 112
(22) Becoming a Wayfarer: Yesterday, Today, and Tomorrow *anonymous* ... 113

(23) Prison Alchemy *by Muhammad Ridá Hisámí (Imprisoned seven years)* 114
(24) True Courage *by Fakhru'd-Dín Húshang Rawhání (Sarkish)* 116
(25) Those Who Keep the Vigil *by Bihrúz Bihishtí* 117
(26) The Code of an Exile in the Cause of God
   by Sálihzádih Samarqandí (died in exile to Siberia) 118
(27) Standing in the Need of Prayer *by 'Abdí* 120
(28) The Cup of Calamity *by Fakhru'd-Dín Húshang Rowhání (Sarkish)* 122
(29) Awjí's Istiqbál of the Mazih Dárad *by Awjí (martyred)* 124
(30) Don the Crimson Robe *by Husayn Qaráchidághí* 125
(31) Song of the Immortal Phoenix *by Dr. Sírús Rowshaní (martyred)* 127
(32) Waiting for Ascent *anonymous* 129
(33) The Fiery Heart *by 'Abdí* 130
(34) A Martyr's Name *by Fakhru'd-Dín Húshang Rawhání (Sarkish)* 131
(35) So Let it Be! *by Manúchihr Hijází* 132
(36) Epitaph *by Fakhru'd-Dín Húshang Rawhání (Sarkish) in memory
   of the martyr 'Atá'u'lláh Yávarí* 133
(37) Entering the Holy City *by Shápúr Markazí (martyred)* 135
(38) Acquiescence to God's Will *by Nábit (martyred)* 137
(39) A Daughter's Dream *In memory of Shídrukh by 'Abdí* 138
(40) Muná *by 'Abdí* 141
(41) The Martyr's Message *by 'Azíz Hakímíyan* 143
(42) In Remembrance: The Free One *by 'Abdí* 144
(43) The Date Palm Laments its Fruit *by 'Abdí* 145
(44) Birds *by 'Abdí* 147
(45) What Do They Want from Us? *by 'Abdí* 148
(46) Meditation Before Death *by Farahmand Muqbilín (Ilhám)* 149
(47) The Terraces of Carmel: In Remembrance of the Báb *anonymous* 151
(48) Abhá *anonymous* 154
(49) Greetings and Salutations, O Írán *by Aqdas Tawfíq (Túskí)* 155
(50) Reunion with the Beloved *by Hushmand Fatheazam* 157

Works Cited 159
Notes 161

Foreword

Who exists in this world who has not at some time partaken of those rays shining forth from the Sun of Love? Whose ears have not now and then heard the murmur of love? Or who of us has not whispered affectionately into the ears of another? The love of a mother for her child, of the lover for the beloved, and the love of the beauty of nature are all but manifestations of the beauty of that eternal love that is manifested in all created things, that love which is the cause of all life and the animating cause of all existent realities.

There is so much about the nature and effects of love in the Bahá'í writings that if these passages were assembled, they would constitute a massive volume indeed. For example, we read in the Bahá'í scriptures that love is the fountainhead of creation, that love is the cause of creation, that love is "the revelation of the Merciful,"[3] that love is "spiritual bounty"[4] and "the cause of the splendors of God in the world of existence."[5] It is "the relationship between God and creation in the realm of soul."[6] And we also read in the Bahá'í texts that through the Divine Will, the Cherished Beloved has cast off the veil, behind which dwells that love emanating from the Essence of God, and that its manifestation and appearance have become the source of all love and yearning and the treasure of all affection and rapture.[7] Furthermore, according to this act of will, the most lofty manifestation of affection is that love which attracts the hearts to the Beloved of Hearts and which forges an eternal bond between ourselves and God, from Whom we emanate and to Whom we all return.

The pages of religious history are full of stories that depict the martyrdom and sacrifice of those preeminent, those chosen people whose hearts became ignited with the flame of faith when, in each successive dispensation, the radiant light of guidance shining forth the fire of the love of God was set ablaze; this is a fire whose heat and power gradually increased until, through its incendiary power, the luminescence of love filled the world so that the eyes of each generation became enlightened by the rays dawning from a new civilization.

In this age, when once again the light of God's incomparable love has, through the Bahá'í Revelation, shed its radiance over the entire world so that the morn of guidance has dawned, plenteous are the stories of the lovers of God who have become drunk with the goblet of that choice wine, who have severed themselves from all save the Beloved, and who have forgotten themselves in the path of His love. The stories of these pure lovers are so revolutionary in their power that they can scarcely be recounted.

How beauteous is the story of that one who, while abandoning his life in the field of martyrdom, smiled when the mocking executioner's sword first struck his taj and knocked it to the ground, and he uttered in response:

> Happy he whom love's intoxication so hath overcome that scarce he knows
> Whether at the feet of the Beloved it be head or turban which he throws![8]

Where else can one find the story of a fiery lover who, as they dragged him to the field of sacrifice – having pierced holes in his shoulders and chest and having placed lit candles in each aperture and having paraded him through alleyways and the bazaar – would in such a state pour forth from his heart-singed soul this melody:

> How I wish that the one who always desired to burn you
> could have come to watch now, if only from a distance.[9]

Where else have we seen or read how oppressors captured and chained a father and his twelve-year-old son, only to slaughter the father before the eyes of his son with atrocious cruelty and then to tell the youth – his breath still sweet-smelling from his mother's milk – that he must leave his Faith if he wishes to avoid his father's fate, only to have this stainless child utter defiantly "Yá Bahá'u'l-Abhá!" (O Thou, the Glory of the Most Glorious) and demand that he be sent quickly to be with his father?

Perhaps some might assume that such events, which occurred more than a hundred years ago, could never come to pass in this modern age. However, the contemporary history of Iran contradicts such assumptions with bare, indisputable facts. For the Bahá'ís in Iran, the birth place of the Bahá'í Faith, have never been free and have never had respite or relief from the hands of cruel fanatics.

Since the recent revolution, the cruelties that have been directed towards the followers of His Holiness Bahá'u'lláh, brought about yet another soul-stirring display of stories of adoration and loyalty onto the world's stage, replicating the same procession of zeal and pain of that previous age, thereby causing the old wine of love to be passed around in a new goblet.

For example, how can one forget those ten guiltless girls in S͟híráz condemned to death, accused without evidence of nothing more than being in love, their only crime being teaching Bahá'í children to have a moral character and good manners. On that day of sacrifice, these brides of the Kingdom were hastening so happily and joyously to the field of martyrdom that it perplexed the hearts of the guards charged with carrying out the sentence of death. One was heard to have said that while

escorting the girls in the bus rumbling towards the place of execution, the girls were so preoccupied with praising God, with chanting prayers, and with intoning melodies and songs, he thought he was taking them to a feast or a celebration.

And when the gallows was ready and the girls were to be hung one at a time in front of the others, each was anxious to go before the others. And when her turn came, each girl took the noose in hand, kissed it, then placed it reverently around her thin neck so that she could ascend by that cord and quickly attain Reunion with the Beloved.

Or how can we not praise that one who was calm and smiling as they took him to the field of martyrdom, then shocked the guards with his laughter when he said, "It is not the bullet that will come toward me! It is I who am rushing towards the bullet!"[10]

These legendary stories have each been recounted by those who have borne witness to these events, or else those who have heard the accounts from people who did. All these accounts have been written down, and, God willing, these authentic documents will in time be collected and published. But what we have in this book through the effort of two Bahá'í scholars – Dr. Amrollah Hemmat, an erudite researcher from Iran, and Dr. John Hatcher, a distinguished literary scholar and poet from America – is a collection and translation of some of the poems that Bahá'í martyrs composed before their execution, describing their own ardor and burning desire in the midst of their separation from the Beloved of the world. Other poems are from those who have been so moved by the stories of those who cast their lives in the path of sacrifice and love, that the gift of verse welled up inside them and empowered them to compose these lines.

This book about poetry and martyrdom is one of the first attempts to enable non-Iranian readers to become familiar with the very delicate feelings that have moved the cherished martyrs of the Bahá'í Faith to risk their lives. This book may well be but a prelude to future volumes penned in other languages as tributes to the memory of those who were consumed by the fire of the love of God.

It is with a thousand regrets and untold remorse that in our world today, as stricken and afflicted as it is with such a stark poverty of spirituality, that delicate human sensibilities that emanate from the divine spirit must remain undisclosed to so many. The human spirit has deviated so far from the path of truth that even cherished words and sounds have lost their essential meaning. The exalted word *love*, that kingly pearl of the treasure of Iranian mystic knowledge and literature, is in these days used in such a base manner that it offends the mind. Consider the word *love* as

it is used in contemporary literature, poetry, and music – it alludes solely to lust and the satisfying of base animal instincts, totally contradicting the verity that "the game of love is one thing, but the worshiping of self is quite another."[11] Likewise, the word *martyrdom* in contemporary society is applied to those who, because of what has been drummed into their minds in the name of religion, lose their lives for inhuman purposes – the killing of the innocent in the name of religious or political causes. They commit these acts with specious promises of an eternal material paradise that will provide them with carnal pleasures and delights, while they utterly abuse another sacred promise.

This is not the concept of martyrdom in the context of the Bahá'í Faith. What Bahá'u'lláh has commanded from his followers is love and affection for all humankind. Furthermore, Bahá'ís do not carry out any act in the hope of paradise or the fear of hell. Even the concept of obedience to Bahá'í law is based on the love of God, not the fear of retribution or the hope of salvation. Bahá'u'lláh says, "Observe My commandments, for the love of My beauty"[12]. And the Báb says, "That which is worthy of His Essence is to worship Him for His sake, without fear of fire, or hope of paradise"[13]. His Holiness 'Abdu'l-Bahá says in one tablet: "The requisite for love is that one would sacrifice his own life for the sake of the Beloved and become a passionate wayfarer disgraced in the eyes of the world."[14] By *sacrifice* in the Bahá'í Faith is not meant that one should intentionally endanger one's life for the sake of reward, or that being slain is inherently a virtue and deserving of reward. Consider the following statement by 'Abdu'l-Bahá:

> This is the time when you should become like a goblet filled to the brim or like the Abhá breeze which bestows life throughout the musk-scented land. Heed not the conditions of the material world, but at every stage of your existence strive only for annihilation. Upon reaching the sun, rays of light become absorbed, and on reaching the sea, a drop loses itself. When attaining the presence of the Beloved, the true lover becomes oblivious to self. For until one has stepped into the station of selflessness, he will be deprived of Divine Bestowals. And it is the path of sacrifice that leads one to the station of nothingness and annihilation wherein divine reality can become manifest. And the end point of sacrifice is the field of detachment wherein the verses of eternity are chanted. Therefore, to the extent that you are able, become totally detached from your self and become enraptured with that Luminous Countenance. And when you attain the station of humility, you will discover that all creation is within your grasp. This is

the Most Great Bounty. This is the Most Great Dominion. This is everlasting life. In the final analysis, all else is but illusion.[15]

No Bahá'í should pursue the goal of endangering himself or losing his life for the hope of achieving the station of martyrdom that thereby he may gain reward. Instead, in the Bahá'í writings we read that martyrdom is acceptable only if it occurs in the course of unforeseen events: that is, if it occurs while one seeks naught but the Beauty of the Friend and treads on naught but the path of love and detachment and loyalty. On this sacred path, if conditions happen such that one needs must offer his life to the Beloved, then of course such sacrifice is acceptable in the Court of Grandeur. But repeatedly in response to the requests of the lovers of His Blessed Beauty who desired to attain martyrdom, His Holiness Bahá'u'lláh advised them that instead of attaining the station of martyrdom, they should arise to render service to the Faith of God and to exert effort in the path of bringing about the unity of humankind, which is the Divine Will for this age – to become living martyrs. Likewise, His Holiness 'Abdu'l-Bahá, in response to a true lover who found the garment of his body too tight and who desired martyrdom, said the following:

> The station of sacrifice is indeed acceptable and admirable, but in this day, one should live in such a way that at each hour he is slain and in each minute he gives up a thousand lives, but martyrdom is losing only one life and then hastening to the realm of the loftiest summit. But it is infinitely more gratifying to sacrifice a hundred thousand lives each moment with the utmost joy and felicity in His Court and to arise in service to God and hasten to the field of courage and guidance, and to scatter before you the ensigns of error and darkness with light from the Dawn of the Divine Unity, and to join forces in the spiritual fray, and to martial an army of mysteries, and to hold aloft the banner of knowledge, and thus to besiege the army of ignorance and folly.[16]

Therefore the martyrs who in this age in Iran, with utmost happiness and bravery, kissed the rope of the gallows or hastened toward the bullets, did so not for the sake of becoming legendary heroes or heroines, nor to be remembered and celebrated. Rather they were so absorbed by the love of God, the Beloved of the world, and were so certain that the path they were treading was naught but the path of love – though it may have sometimes required bloodshed, it was exhilarating – that they knew that by sacrificing their lives, they would demonstrate their love to the world of humanity. And since they listened to the message of the call from the Realm of the Invisible, they also knew that love and affection in the spiritual realm are like life to the body in this mortal world.

Indeed, in this mutable life of ours, love causes nations to become civilized. It is the cause of the progress of humanity. That is why, with utmost detachment – which is the sign of faith – these enraptured souls shone forth from the dawning place of sacrifice. And even if the hands of the oppressors had not been stained with their blood, most of them would likely have dwelled in this mortal world but a while longer. For not only did these believers, burning with the fire of the love of God, establish a firm foundation and reason for being in love, they also searched for perfection in love, and having found that love, hastened to the kingdom of eternity.

We Iranians who have witnessed in the past and who are still witnessing the sacrifice of our dear ones should be extremely thankful to Mr. Hemmat and Mr. Hatcher who, by translating and publishing these poems related to the mystery of sacrifice, have stirred our hearts to remember those who now reside in the realm of eternity. What is more, they have enabled those who are not Iranians (whether Bahá'ís or not) to gain an insight into something quite alien to common experience, an insight which, one can only hope, will stir in the hearts of the readers both empathy and gratitude.

Hushmand Fatheazam

Preface

It is well known that during the first two epochs of the Heroic Age of the Bahá'í Faith[17] (from 1844 to 1892) the Bahá'ís in Persia and in the Ottoman Empire[18] suffered atrocious persecution at the hands of the theocratically aligned regimes under the Sháhs of Persia, particularly under the notorious Násiri'd-Dín Sháh, and under the Sultans of the Ottoman Empire, most notably Sultan 'Abdu'l-'Azíz.

More than twenty thousand Bahá'ís were executed, often after a type of humiliation and torture unthinkable and unknown in the West. These acts were so heinous that European observers marveled in disbelief at the heroism of these martyrs and at the brutality of the oppressors. Some chronicled these events in vivid and gory detail, some excerpts from which can be studied in Nabíl's narrative *The Dawn-Breakers*.[19]

Ever since then, the Bahá'í community in Iran has been the target of persecution and prejudice, though in the latter part of the 20th century, the more overt forms of this oppression had somewhat relented. But with the triumph of the Islamic revolution in 1979, the persecution of Bahá'ís intensified as the fundamentalist Islamic regime embarked on a systematic campaign to eradicate the Bahá'í community of Iran. Between 1978 and 1998, more than 200 Bahá'ís were executed by the Iranian Government, and the majority of these were the elected members of the councils of the Bahá'í Faith – the Local and National Spiritual Assemblies.

During the 1980s Bahá'ís were imprisoned or else subjected to other forms of deprivation, such as loss of jobs and educational opportunities, all simply because they were followers of the Bahá'í Faith. These oppressive measures continue largely unabated, in spite of protests from the international community.

This book is dedicated to the heroic members of the Bahá'í community in Iran, most especially those who choose execution rather than recanting their belief in Bahá'u'lláh, the Prophet and Founder of the Bahá'í Faith. Some of the poems in this volume are penned by those who were martyred. Other poems are written by Bahá'ís who were friends of these martyrs or who pay tribute to the heroic actions of these figures.

What is Martyrdom?

In recent years, peoples of the contemporary world have become acquainted with a concept of *martyrdom* which constitutes an act of aggression and self-sacrifice as a

type of offensive weapon. While this military technique was employed by the Japanese kamikaze pilots in World War II against American naval vessels, the more recent attacks have been aimed at innocent civilian populations in the Middle East, in America, and in other parts of the world to assert religious and political objectives.

Even though these acts are often committed out of religious devotion or patriotic fervor, the result of this brutality is that the concept of martyrdom has taken on the connotation of fanaticism with the purpose of destroying the lives of innocent civilians in order to disrupt social order and, in some cases, to prevent the progress of efforts to establish peaceful reconciliation among various political interests.

However noble some may deem them, these suicidal attacks do not comply with the traditional concept of what constitutes martyrdom, especially in terms of religious history. According to the accepted definition, a martyr is one who "chooses to suffer death rather than renounce religious principles."[20] And it is this definition of martyrdom and oppression to which this collection of verse alludes – unsought victimization resulting from a refusal to recant one's beliefs or to accept the imposition of a creed contrary to one's faith.

We do not mean to imply by these observations that none of the contemporary "suicide bombers" are without what they sincerely believe to be sacred or legitimate goals. We will leave it to the judgment of an Omniscient Deity to assay the ultimate motive behind any of these acts to determine to what extent these sacrifices constitute acts of piety or devotion. But clearly the term martyr as it has been applied down through the ages and as we will employ it in this work alludes exclusively to those who are not soldiers, who are not adversaries, and who have no intention of causing harm to others.

What is more, since it is Bahá'í law that every believer abide by the laws of the land in which he or she lives, Bahá'ís behave as loyal and faithful citizens. They are forbidden to become involved in partisan or divisive political issues. As a result, the people whose lives are celebrated or commemorated in this volume are remarkable for the purity of their conduct, for the refinement of their character, and not merely for their obvious courage in the face of fatal choices.

This is not to say that these Bahá'í martyrs are absolutely passive. They forthrightly assert their right to think and believe as they see fit, and they articulate what they believe to be the principles of an authentic religion of God, the Bahá'í Faith. But they in no wise attempt to impose these beliefs on others. Indeed, proselytizing is contrary to the Bahá'í teachings, as is any sort of aggression against those who would deny or denounce these beliefs. Finally, it is well worth noting that some

religions permit believers to give lip denial of faith in times of peril. For example, in Shí'ih Islam this practice is termed taqíyyih. But the laws of the Bahá'í Faith explicitly forbid the recanting of one's faith, even in life-threatening situations.

The reader is free to decide who is and who is not deserving of the appellation martyr or what exactly the term martyr implies. What we do know is that individuals who penned the verses in this volume, either as a prelude to their own execution or as poetic tributes to those souls who made the ultimate sacrifice, are alluding to the torture and subsequent execution of individuals who intended no harm to anyone and no rebellion against civil law or authority. They simply refused to renounce what they believed to be true and refused to accept beliefs against their will.

The Muslim Rationale

Since the Qur'án states unequivocally that religion should not be imposed on others, one might well wonder why the Bahá'ís have been systematically persecuted in Iran and throughout other Islamic countries in the Middle East for more than a century. This question is especially warranted since in the Qur'án Muhammad specifically describes all religions as part of a continuous divine process of educating humankind and since He specifically admonishes His followers, "Let there be no compulsion in religion"[21].

One important answer can be found in a particular passage in the Qur'án which many Muslims believe to imply that God would send no further Prophets or Apostles after Muhammad, "Muhammad is not the father of any of your men, but [he is] the Messenger of Allah, and the Seal of the Prophets: and Allah has full knowledge of all things."[22]

Some feel there are obvious refutations of a literalist interpretation of the symbolic term *seal*.[23] For example, the word *khátam* denotes *end*, at least in contemporary Arabic. But the word also alludes to a *ring*, as in a seal ring used by men of prominence in the past to stamp their name or symbol at the end of their letters to assure the recipient that the epistle was authentic. But the fact is that in either interpretation, the concept of finality can be legitimately inferred from the passage.

Thus, where one might argue that the term *seal* in this passage means that Muhammad has the authentic properties of Prophethood, as had those Apostles that preceded him, Bahá'u'lláh's explanation about the confusion regarding this critical passage and its abuse focuses on two other aspects of the term.

First Bahá'u'lláh acknowledges that the term has been indeed misunderstood in such a way that it has deterred many Muslims from recognizing the fact that Divine revelation is and always will be a continuous process:

> It hath been demonstrated and definitely established, through clear evidences, that by "Resurrection" is meant the rise of the Manifestation of God to proclaim His Cause, and by "attainment unto the divine Presence" is meant attainment unto the presence of His Beauty in the person of His Manifestation. For verily, "No vision taketh in Him, but He taketh in all vision." Notwithstanding all these indubitable facts and lucid statements, they [some Muslims clerics] have foolishly clung to the term "seal," and remained utterly deprived of the recognition of Him Who is the Revealer of both the Seal and the Beginning, in the day of His presence.[24]

In one explanation of the term, Bahá'u'lláh observes that every Prophet manifests the *seal* of Prophethood, both in His person and in His revelation. That is, the Prophets can be recognized by Their *sunna*,[25] Their *person*[26] or example, and the pattern of perfection in Their daily lives. But more to the point, Bahá'u'lláh in the *Kitáb-i-Íqán* notes that all the Prophets or Apostles of God partake of the attributes of being the "first" and the "last":

> From these statements therefore it hath been made evident and manifest that should a Soul in the "End that knoweth no end" be made manifest, and arise to proclaim and uphold a Cause which in "the Beginning that hath no beginning" another Soul had proclaimed and upheld, it can be truly declared of Him Who is the Last and of Him Who was the First that they are one and the same, inasmuch as both are the Exponents of one and the same Cause. For this reason, hath the Point of the Bayán - may the life of all else but Him be His sacrifice! - likened the Manifestations of God unto the sun which, though it rise from the "Beginning that hath no beginning" until the "End that knoweth no end," is none the less the same sun. Now, wert thou to say, that this sun is the former sun, thou speakest the truth; and if thou sayest that this sun is the "return" of that sun, thou also speakest the truth. Likewise, from this statement it is made evident that the term "last" is applicable to the "first," and the term "first" applicable to the "last;" inasmuch as both the "first" and the "last" have risen to proclaim one and the same Faith.[27]

In this sense, every Prophet partakes of the attribute of being the *seal* of the Prophets, a point which Bahá'u'lláh immediately discusses after the preceding passage:

> Notwithstanding the obviousness of this theme, in the eyes of those that have quaffed the wine of knowledge and certitude, yet how many are those who, through failure to understand its meaning, have allowed the term "Seal of the Prophets" to obscure their understanding, and deprive them of the grace of all His manifold bounties! Hath not Muhammad, Himself, declared: "I am all the Prophets?" Hath He not said as We have already mentioned: "I am Adam, Noah, Moses, and Jesus?" Why should Muhammad, that immortal Beauty, Who hath said: "I am the first Adam" be incapable of saying also: "I am the last Adam?" For even as He regarded Himself to be the "First of the Prophets" - that is Adam - in like manner, the "Seal of the Prophets" is also applicable unto that Divine Beauty. It is admittedly obvious that being the "First of the Prophets," He likewise is their "Seal."[28]

Of course, this explanation is not simple to follow unless one truly understands the concept of the station and ontology of the Manifestations, something which we can not fully explicate here. Suffice it to say that, in addition to the preceding explanation, Bahá'u'lláh also affirms that inasmuch as Muhammad represents the last Prophet in the Prophetic or Adamic cycle, He is indeed the last Prophet before the Day of Resurrection so often discussed in the Qur'án, an event which Bahá'ís believe occurred with the appearance of the Báb in 1844.

That is, the Báb as the "Primal Point" represents the confluence of two cycles – the end of the Adamic Cycle and the beginning of the Bahá'í Era. In this sense, Muhammad is the last of those Apostles who prepared humankind through prophecy for this critical point of change in the evolution of human society on the planet, what the Bahá'í texts describe as the maturation of humankind. In the following passage, Shoghi Effendi quotes from Bahá'u'lláh's allusion to the fact that the time for the maturation of humankind has at long last arrived:

> "The world," He proclaims, "is but one country, and mankind its citizens." He further affirms that the unification of mankind, the last stage in the evolution of humanity towards maturity is inevitable, that "soon will the present day order be rolled up, and a new one spread out in its stead," that "the whole earth is now in a state of pregnancy," that "the day is approaching when it will have yielded its noblest fruits, when from it will have

sprung forth the loftiest trees, the most enchanting blossoms, the most heavenly blessings."[29]

Thus the Báb, as the Qá'im, fulfills the promises of both the Qur'án and the authentic Islamic traditions that all would be fulfilled with the Day of Resurrection of humankind, and hence this point in history has been anticipated by all the Manifestations throughout the Adamic cycle, most prominently by Muhammad, the "Seal" of the Prophets for that preparatory cycle in human history:

> He [the Báb] is the Revealer of the divine mysteries, and the Expounder of the hidden and ancient wisdom. Thus it is related in the "Biháru'l-Anvár," the "Aválim," and the "Yanbu'" of Sádiq, son of Muhammad, that he spoke these words: "Knowledge is twenty and seven letters. All that the Prophets have revealed are two letters thereof. No man thus far hath known more than these two letters. But when the Qá'im shall arise, He will cause the remaining twenty and five letters to be made manifest." Consider; He hath declared Knowledge to consist of twenty and seven letters, and regarded all the Prophets, from Adam even unto the "Seal," as Expounders of only two letters thereof and of having been sent down with these two letters. He also saith that the Qá'im will reveal all the remaining twenty and five letters. Behold from this utterance how great and lofty is His station! His rank excelleth that of all the Prophets, and His Revelation transcendeth the comprehension and understanding of all their chosen ones.[30]

But possibly the most important proof that Muhammad is not asserting that there will be no further revelation from God is that we can hardly accept the idea that a loving God would at some given point in the progress of human society suddenly cease bestowing guidance, any more than a parent would at some point cease to assist his or her own offspring. For if human beings are by definition endlessly perfectible, both individually and collectively, how could this process of producing an "ever-advancing civilization"[31] suddenly become finished or finalized?

So it is that the human race will always need further information and further guidance because we never achieve some final stage of development. Thus, the term *seal* does indeed signal that something is completed or finished – a particular period in the ever-evolving education of humankind on this planet. But regardless of what logic one might use to support any form of Islamic chauvinism, suffice it to say that while there exists in the Qur'án the nominal sanction of the religions revealed previous to Islam (e.g., Judaism and Christianity), any religion based on the belief that a Prophet has appeared since Muhammad is generally not tolerated by

those Muslims who believe that there will be no further revelations after the appearance of Muhammad.

As a result, the Bahá'í Faith, which claims that a revelation occurred in 1844 (ergo, since the time of Muhammad in 622 A.D.), is deemed to be committing apostasy by most Middle Eastern Muslim clerics. On this basis, or at least using this argument as an excuse to deter the growing appeal of the Bahá'í religion, Bahá'ís have been systematically condemned as enemies of the Faith of Islam, as heretics or "infidels." Furthermore, because the world center of the Bahá'í community is located in Israel, the Muslim countries have sometimes attempted to portray the Bahá'í Faith as supporting "Zionism" and the Bahá'ís themselves as "spies" for Israel.

But this scriptural rationale and this political motive have most often been employed only by those who feel some need to justify their actions. In fact, much of the persecution has had purely personal motives. Religion and alliance with religious leaders has been a principal means by which the governments involved could maintain political control, particularly over the less educated masses who would tend to follow blindly the dictates of those clerics whom they consider to be more learned and astute than themselves. Governments have thus found in the Bahá'í community useful scapegoats to distract public attention from economic and social ills.

In addition, the Bahá'í religion places great emphasis on the importance of education and social progress. Consequently, Bahá'ís are almost inevitably among the most educated, successful and ambitious members the communities in which they live. Therefore, when there is social discord or upheaval, the Bahá'ís are easy targets, especially since all one has to determine if one is a Bahá'ís is ask.

Thus, while some of the poems in this volume are from or about famous historical figures who lived over a century ago, during the time of Bahá'u'lláh and 'Abdu'l-Bahá (e.g., Varqá and his son Rúhu'lláh), other poems concern figures who have been executed since the overthrow of the Sháh in 1979. This relatively recent and unexpected reversal of fortunes for the Bahá'í community of Iran, which had for some time achieved recognition and esteem in various fields of learning and business there, made the worldwide Bahá'í community suddenly take note that what many of them had considered to be the almost mythical history of the early martyrs was all too real and not confined to a single historical period nor to specialized individuals. Suddenly the contemporary Bahá'ís in Iran were being forced to make this same critical choice – to renounce their Faith and accept Islam, or to be tortured and executed.

The entire National Spiritual Assembly at the time (1979) was kidnapped and its members are now presumed dead. Soon all Bahá'í private property and fortunes were seized. Civil rights were suspended, even the right to education. Appeals were made by Bahá'í communities worldwide to national governments and to the United Nations to intervene. While these protests had important effects, the persecution continues to this day.

Thus, the oppression and martyrdom alluded to in this collection of verse does not merely imply physical torture or execution in the name of a system of belief. These poems describe the forsaking of all else to serve a specific spiritual purpose – the advancement of the welfare of humankind by remaining faithful to the divine plan revealed by Bahá'u'lláh which, Bahá'ís believe, is the means by which the salvation of humankind can occur.

The motive of those who have endured and are enduring these privations is, therefore, not to attain personal status, either among those left behind in the material world who remember and celebrate the martyr's name, or among the heavenly hosts who may welcome the brave soul into their midst. Instead, these poems present the Bahá'í perspective of the planet as a global community, something made especially clear by a poem toward the end of the volume by an individual who is not a Bahá'í.

Finally, it is extremely important to note that the Bahá'í Writings forbid seeking martyrdom. Furthermore, these same scriptures exalt service to humankind to the rank of sacrificing one's life. This does not mean Bahá'ís do not deem the free choice of deciding whether or not to recant one's beliefs as a supreme test of one's certitude. Indeed, not all those tested have been able to hold fast to the "firm cord."[32] Bahá'ís certainly deem martyrdom a supreme sacrifice, yet not necessarily the only sacrifice worthy of praise and exaltation.

Martyrdom is, in its most refined sense, a value judgment in action, the supreme test of conviction in one's assertions about the spiritual meaning of this life. And yet, sacrificing one's life may not be the most difficult or significant contribution one can make, either to religious conviction or to the betterment of humankind. One might correctly conclude that living a long life of daily struggle and unrelenting attention to one's spiritual growth and development as expressed in countless acts of selfless devotion and service is no less noble.

Certainly A *Daughter's Dream about Her Mother* brings to the foreground this very issue, as does the final poem in an oblique way. For the Bahá'í, overcoming self in order to become a refined member of the human family is possibly the most

important contribution one can make to the advancement of the principles set forth by Bahá'u'lláh.

In the well-known Tablet of Ahmad, Bahá'u'lláh summons the true believer to teach others the truth of the Cause of God, stating that the mere chanting of the exhortation contained in this teaching tablet will result in the "reward of a hundred martyrs": "Learn well this Tablet, O Ahmad. Chant it during thy days and withhold not thyself therefrom. For verily, God hath ordained for the one who chants it, the reward of a hundred martyrs and a service in both worlds."[33]

In a study of this tablet in *The Ocean of His Words*, we find the assertion that one possible meaning of this promise might be that one who arises to teach the Cause of God will receive the reward of being assisted by a hundred souls who have already ascended to the Abhá Kingdom after making the ultimate sacrifice. Likewise, the concept of the reward of service being more service, both in this world and in the afterlife, is a major conclusion of this volume, even as the now deceased martyr says to her daughter in *A Daughter's Dream about Her Mother*:

> Daughter, true you are now from the proud lineage of martyrs,
> but know that the heritage I bequeathed you is even greater,
> for in the lofty place where dwell the angels on high
> a choral cry calls out from thirty thousand martyrs:
> 'Though the station of martyrdom bequeathed by the
>   Friend's benevolence
> is a glorious robe of honor, a crown of great felicity,
> the act of arising to serve His Cause with selflessness and sincerity
> is a rank higher and more lofty than the station of martyrdom itself!'

Thus, a life of service ultimately may be equivalent to the sacrifice of one's life, or, indeed, may require the incremental sacrificing of one's life. This verity is especially meaningful if by sacrifice we recall the Latin root of the word which means "to make sacred."

The Poems as Art

We have chosen poems that have merit, though not all the poems in this volume are necessarily great works of art. Our primary criterion for selecting these poems has been the power of their content. At times these verses were written as Bahá'ís faced the ultimate challenge, not simply of remaining faithful to their beliefs, but also of coming to terms with the deepest meaning of this act – leaving behind family

and loved ones. The true power of some of these pieces often lies in their capacity to demystify this heroic act by allowing us to glimpse the internal process of the hero or heroine who is, after all, an ordinary human being in extraordinary circumstances.

These glimpses into the psyche of the martyr are sometimes more meaningful and more revealing than the elliptical stories that are told of mythic Bahá'í heroes like Táhirih, Mullá Husayn, Quddús, Hujjat, or Vahíd. In the poem by Shapúr Markazí, for example, we experience the willful transition in this martyr's attitude from that of a grieving father saying farewell to his beloved children who have come to his prison cell to pay one last visit, to that of a determined and fearless believer consciously and willfully setting aside his earthly concerns and affections to seize the cord of certitude. We sense in his words the willful summoning of courage sufficient to receive the mantle of martyrdom with honor and dignity:

> I embraced firmly those so dear
> to my heart and soul until the guard
> pronounced the ultimate pain:
> This was farewell!
> My burning heart became inflamed with sorrow,
> the herald of a thousand further sorrows.
> Light left my eyes as my soul
> departed from my breast:
> "These precious two are my life, my existence!
> There is no further need of
> waiting at the door. Have I nothing left
> but privation and despair?"
> Trust, O Heart, in the benevolence of the Beloved!
> Pray that your life will soon
> depart this shell,
> that you may become a sacrifice
> for His Holiness, the Beloved, and no longer abide
> with these bleak companions, Pain and Despair!
> Entrust your dear ones to God
> then follow the brave path,
> O you who claim to believe!

In other poems, we witness the martyr having already attained that state of willing resignation to his or her fate, and relishing the opportunity to sacrifice all for the sake of the Beloved. In still other poems, the emphasis or theme focuses not on the

singular event of an individual being slaughtered, or even on the oppression and deprivation which the believers as a whole have endured, but on the long-term impact of these events on the ultimate redemption of humankind.

The Structure of the Volume

We have structured the sequence of poems in both parts of *Reunion with the Beloved* to emphasize the ultimately felicitous outcome of these unfortunate events in terms of Bahá'í history and, even more importantly, in terms of the progress of our global community towards unity and peace, the theme which is at the heart of Bahá'u'lláh's Revelation and all that the Bahá'í Faith endeavors to foster. Therefore, the poems at the end of both sections are filled with hope, not thoughts of despair or revenge. The ultimate vision of this volume is the redemption of the country of Iran and its people, and the unification of the planet as one integrated community.

Insofar as the translations of these poems are concerned, we have rendered the traditional Persian form of rhymed couplets either as couplets or, in the case of poems with longer lines, as quatrains. The quatrain is a natural form for translating the couplets, because most have a caesura or pause, either syntactical or semantic, in the middle of the lines. Some of the poems in Part II are modern and do not employ couplets. These we have rendered more freely, even as the poet intended. Consequently, the translation for these modern verses will not always follow precisely line for line.

Not all the poems are by Bahá'ís or by Bahá'ís who were martyred. Furthermore, four of the poems are anonymous in the sources from which we have taken them.[34] We have grouped the poems into two periods according to whether they were by or about the Heroic Age of the Faith (1844-1921) or about the persecution that has occurred since the revolution in Iran in 1979. If the poem is penned by someone who was martyred, we have so indicated in parenthesis beneath the author's name.

The similarity between the thoughts expressed in these two sections is remarkable, even though the events associated with these periods are separated by almost a century. In both sections one can detect a growing sense of detachment from physical reality, an emotion which eventually evolves into an eagerness to leave the material world. The end result of this process is the act of martyrdom itself as reflected in accounts of these events, followed at the conclusion of both sections by poems that meditate on the overall purpose and effect of these sacrifices in advancing the Cause of God.

The volume in its totality is thus a depiction of one's journey to the heights of spiritual destiny, and the unfolding drama of the struggles, tests and victories in this adventurous journey.

The volume begins with God calling man to a festive reunion and ends with man's longing for reunion with God, a station which is impossible except through striving for selflessness and humble service. The first poem by Na'ím concerns God calling man to the spiritual heights in the midst of war and strife. The voice beckons humankind towards peace and delight by making sacrifices for the lofty objective of the unity of mankind.

Varqá, in the poem that follows reminds one to respond to God's call and delineates in some detail how the wayfarer should tread this path. In the next poem, Varqá gives examples of the many lovers of Truth by alluding to the saints and prophets who responded to God's call by offering up their undefiled lives in the path of God. Varqá thus sees responding to God's call as a universal phenomenon:

> There is no heart that is not feverish in Your path;
> there is no eye that is not crying in longing for You.
> Anywhere there exists a heart, it is heavy with blood because of You;
> Anywhere there exists a mind, it is perplexed, bewildered because of You.

The three poems that follow are ecstatic expressions by Varqá and others of their personal desire and longing for sacrifice, even to the point of martyrdom:

> I have no fear of being slaughtered
> in His quarter:
> the sacrifice of this lifeless bird
> would be delightful.

Rúhu'lláh's mathnaví is also an account of his desire for release from the prison of physical life: "Help O King of the Kingdom of the souls/ my heart is aflame in its remoteness from you… rescue this bird from the snare of despondency."

The prayers of Rúhu'lláh and his father Varqá are answered, and the details of the events of their martyrdom are depicted in the language of doves in "Tears of the Dove." There follows the moving eulogy penned by Nayyir and Síná, a poem that was praised by 'Abdu'l-Bahá:

> Alas, Alas, O Land of Tá,[35]
> what has happened to Varqá? Where is he,[36]
> that dove of the garden of Abhá Beauty?
> What befell him?

The poems that follow are reflections on the martyrdom and sacrifices of the heroic age: "The story of these lovers shall eclipse from our memories/ the fable of Majnún and the legend of Farhád," Na'ím proclaims. In the last two poems of Part One Na'ím reminds us that the purpose of all these sacrifices is the unity of mankind. He declares that the time for unity and accord has at long last arrived and the Master's setting foot on America's shore is a sign of the advent of the amity of mankind.

Part Two is an account of a more recent saga, a resurgence of persecutions in the latter decades of the twentieth century. In the first poem 'Abdí pleads with the fanatic Muslims not to resume their atrocities again, but in the poem that follows he gives up on his useless plea: "O Shaykh, strike as repeatedly as you wish with your taunts, with arrows of oppression upon the caravan of Bahá'ís." The poem following, "Seize the 'Sure Handle,'" responds to the same threats, but with a dauntless courage to endure:

> Do not threaten us with
> the wave's tumult or storm's surge:
> If the water has already surged above our heads,
> we will have no fear of the sea.

The following poems reflect on the early histories of martyrdom, on the believers' detachment from the limitations of the physical world, and on the eternal spiritual destiny that awaits these believers. Among the most incisive are those poems that meditate on the true internal freedom that one may achieve in spite of physical imprisonment and on the certitude and resolve of the true believer in spite of tests and difficulties:

> Even should the world itself
> sink into a stormy maelstrom,
> I will be like Noah and never drown
> in the fathomless ocean of storms

Various pieces portray the believer's detachment and readiness for sacrifice, and, as the sequence progresses, this attitude of detachment gradually evolves into a longing for sacrifice, the climax of this tone being those pieces that characterize

the believer's anticipation of freedom from this nether world. At last there emerges something beyond mere readiness; the poems express an unquenchable eagerness for martyrdom:

> Happy shall be the day I withdraw
> my hands from both wet and dry
> and like flames my head will rise
> in the blessed air of the Friend.

Then follow depictions of the drama of martyrdom itself – the martyr's conversation with the executioner, the shedding of the blood of the innocent, and the emblazoning of a martyr's name on the door of paradise. In one piece the believer responds to this grievous event with ironic acquiescence to his execution: "The soul in its dance flew to paradise, So be it!"

After this portrayal of martyrdoms are poems that contain accounts of several recent martyrs, either in the martyr's own language or by those who remember them: their longing for sacrifice, their hesitation and confusion of mind, the effects of their sacrifices on the world and on those who, while exiled from their homeland, continue to hear sad news of their beloved friends being executed. For example, 'Abdí desperately cries out:

> I know not what these people desire from us?
> What else do they desire from these captives of calamity?
> What do they want?

The concluding poems allude to the ultimately glorious outcome of these sacrifices in the progress of human history. The martyrdom of the Báb has led to Mount Carmel becoming a Tabernacle for the unity of all mankind. A Muslim expresses love for Bahá'u'lláh and regrets what the fanatics in his Faith have done to Bahá'u'lláh's native land. The final poem by retired Universal House of Justice member, Húshmand Fatheazam, expresses the soul's desire for reunion with the Friend, but concludes with the realization that each individual is charged with a distinct task in responding to God's call, whether that response be expressed in the dramatic sacrifice of one's life or in daily attention to continuously striving for selflessness in the path of servitude:

> Thus will I become dust in His path, and the Beloved will pass by,
> that traceless Friend so unlike any other in the world.
> O my heart, glad tidings to you! Attaining reunion with the Friend
> is not remote at all from the beneficence of that Kind One!

SOME CULTURAL INSIGHTS

Poetry, being an art form, can sometimes offer a glimpse into the innermost thoughts and consciousness of people in a way that cannot be discovered or disclosed through the mass media or even through day-to-day interaction with people. Naturally, understanding a culture different from our own is always a difficult task – to the degree that it is possible at all. To go beyond the filtering of information and the subtle coloring that results from media bias, one needs to face the most intimate emotional life of the people. Poetry, particularly poetry penned in the heat of passion, pain and fatal choices, can help communicate this insight.

Since this collection contains some poems by contemporary Persian Bahá'í poets, the book is also of value to those interested in the present condition in the Middle East, to academics in such disciplines as anthropology, literature, Islamic studies, and religion, as well as to anyone interested in obtaining a deeper understanding of contemporary Iran. But to the English-speaking Bahá'í community we hope this collection will make a special contribution. In spite of great concern for their co-religionists in Iran, the English-speaking Bahá'ís, by and large, are not in touch with the deepest thoughts and feelings of the Bahá'í community of Iran. The wealth of Persian literature, stories, poems, and articles published during the last two decades have not been translated into English. Only news of persecutions and appeals for help have been communicated.

The very difficult and delicate task of translating the literature and poetry of Persian Bahá'ís remains to be addressed, and we hope this collection will make a beginning by helping to develop a deeper and stronger integration of the Persian Bahá'ís into the communities in which they have settled around the world as a result of these religious persecutions or else as a result of their pursuit of spiritual or academic goals.

By focusing on Bahá'í Persian poets, this volume does not portray a glimpse of Iran or of the Islamic culture as a whole. It does demonstrate the hopes, the fears, the aspirations, the brave struggles, and the intellectuality of the Bahá'í minority. Perhaps this volume will enable the English-speaking world to become more aware of and empathetic with the pain and the heroic resistance of this minority that

thereby readers may be prompted to assist the international Bahá'í community in putting an end to the ceaseless persecutions that have plagued this religion since its inception more than 160 years ago.

The reader should be reminded that the natural emphasis of the poems on the persecutions of Bahá'ís should not lead one to the conclusion that the generality of the non-Bahá'í community in Iran is in favor of such discrimination and cruelties. We have translated the poem Abhá, a poem by a non-Bahá'í contemporary poet, to demonstrate the sympathy and admiration that many non-Bahá'í Iranians have for their fellow Bahá'í countrymen.

Likewise, one should not infer from these poems that Islam itself advocates the unjust and unfair practices of many Iranian government agents and clerics during the last 160 years. In fact, the recent apology made by the Pope for the unfair and cruel treatment of the Jewish community by the Catholics during World War II demonstrates how a large community, along with its organizations and religious structure, can deviate from the most important teachings of their faith.

Finally, should the reader want access to more specific details about the history of the events alluded to by these poems, a good place to begin might be several books that give details about this history: Shoghi Effendi, ed. and trans., *The Dawn-Breakers: Nabíl's Narrative of the Early Days of the Bahá'í Revelation* (Wilmette, IL, Bahá'í Publishing Trust, 1962) in its entirety for accounts of the persecutions from 1844 to 1852; Shoghi Effendi, *God Passes By* (Wilmette, IL: Bahá'í Publishing Trust, 1974) for accounts from 1852 to 1944; and *The Bahá'í Question: Iran's Secret Blueprint for the Destruction of a Religious Community* (New York: Bahá'í International Community Publications, 1999) for accounts dealing with persecution from 1979 to 1999.

Rúhu'lláh

Part I: Kings Among Kings[37]

Background

The face of Rúhu'lláh is resolute, calm, fearless. The hands are still those of a child, a twelve-year-old boy. The eyes see beyond the camera. They penetrate into our hearts with a vision of reality quite beyond anything we have ever witnessed. He has not yet witnessed his father, Varqá, slashed to pieces before his eyes. He has not yet been asked the fatal question, but in his mind the answer has been fashioned into words he had already penned in a poem of longing to be united with his Beloved.

The Battle at Fort Shaykh Tabarsí[38]   *An excerpt from* ***God Passes By***

The Báb's captivity in a remote corner of Ádhirbayján, immortalized by the proceedings of the Conference of Badasht, and distinguished by such notable developments as the public declaration of His mission, the formulation of the laws of His Dispensation and the establishment of His Covenant, was to acquire added significance through the dire convulsions that sprang from the acts of both His adversaries and His disciples. The commotions that ensued, as the years of that captivity drew to a close, and that culminated in His own martyrdom, called forth a degree of heroism on the part of His followers and a fierceness of hostility on the part of His enemies which had never been witnessed during the first three years of His ministry. Indeed, this brief but most turbulent period may be rightly regarded as the bloodiest and most dramatic of the Heroic Age of the Bahá'í Era....

For the first time in the Faith's history a systematic campaign in which the civil and ecclesiastical powers were banded together was being launched against it, a campaign that was to culminate in the horrors experienced by Bahá'u'lláh in the Síyáh-Chál of Tihrán and His subsequent banishment to Iraq. Government, clergy and people arose, as one man, to assault and exterminate their common enemy. In remote and isolated centers the scattered disciples of a persecuted community were pitilessly struck down by the sword of their foes, while in centers where large numbers had congregated measures were taken in self-defense, which, misconstrued by a cunning and deceitful adversary, served in their turn to inflame still further the hostility of the authorities, and multiply the outrages perpetrated by the oppressor. In the East at Shaykh Tabarsí, in the south in Nayríz, in the west in Zanján, and in the capital itself, massacres, upheavals, demonstrations, engagements, sieges and

acts of treachery proclaimed, in rapid succession, the violence of the storm which had broken out, and exposed the bankruptcy, and blackened the annals, of a proud yet degenerate people.

The audacity of Mullá Husayn who, at the command of the Báb, had attired his head with the green turban worn and sent to him by his Master, who had hoisted the Black Standard, the unfurling of which would, according to the Prophet Muhammad, herald the advent of the viceregent of God on earth, and who, mounted on his steed, was marching at the head of two hundred and two of his fellow-disciples to meet and lend his assistance to Quddús in the Jazíriy-i-Khadrá (Verdant Isle)--his audacity was the signal for a clash the reverberations of which were to resound throughout the entire country. The contest lasted no less than eleven months. Its theatre was for the most part the forest of Mazindarán. Its heroes were the flower of the Báb's disciples. Its martyrs comprised no less than half of the Letters of the Living, not excluding Quddús and Mullá Husayn, respectively the last and the first of these Letters. The directive force which, however unobtrusively, sustained it, was none other than that which flowed from the mind of Bahá'u'lláh. It was caused by the unconcealed determination of the dawn-breakers of a new Age to proclaim, fearlessly and befittingly, its advent, and by a no less unyielding resolve, should persuasion prove a failure, to resist and defend themselves against the onslaughts of malicious and unreasoning assailants. It demonstrated beyond the shadow of a doubt what the indomitable spirit of a band of three hundred and thirteen untrained, unequipped yet God-intoxicated students, mostly sedentary recluses of the college and cloister, could achieve when pitted in self-defense against a trained army, well-equipped, supported by the masses of the people, blessed by the clergy, headed by a prince of the royal blood, backed by the resources of the state, acting with the enthusiastic approval of its sovereign, and animated by the unfailing counsels of a resolute and all-powerful minister. Its outcome was a heinous betrayal ending in an orgy of slaughter, staining with everlasting infamy its perpetrators, investing its victims with a halo of imperishable glory, and generating the very seeds which, in a later age, were to blossom into world-wide administrative institutions, and which must, in the fullness of time, yield their golden fruit in the shape of a world-redeeming, earth-encircling Order.

It will be unnecessary to attempt even an abbreviated narrative of this tragic episode, however grave its import, however much misconstrued by adverse chroniclers and historians. A glance over its salient features will suffice for the purpose of these pages. We note, as we conjure up the events of this great tragedy, the fortitude, the intrepidity, the discipline and the resourcefulness of its heroes, contrasting sharply

with the turpitude, the cowardice, the disorderliness and the inconstancy of their opponents. We observe the sublime patience, the noble restraint exercised by one of its principal actors, the lion-hearted Mullá Husayn, who persistently refused to unsheathe his sword until an armed and angry multitude, uttering the foulest invectives, had gathered at a farsang's distance from Barfurúsh to block his way, and had mortally struck down seven of his innocent and staunch companions. We are filled with admiration for the tenacity of faith of that same Mullá Husayn, demonstrated by his resolve to persevere in sounding the adhán, while besieged in the caravanserai of Sabsih-Maydán, though three of his companions, who had successively ascended to the roof of the inn, with the express purpose of performing that sacred rite, had been instantly killed by the bullets of the enemy. We marvel at the spirit of renunciation that prompted those sore pressed sufferers to contemptuously ignore the possessions left behind by their fleeing enemy; that led them to discard their own belongings, and content themselves with their steeds and swords; that induced the father of Badí, one of that gallant company, to fling unhesitatingly by the roadside the satchel, full of turquoises which he had brought from his father's mine in Nishápúr; that led Mírzá Muhammad-Taqíy-i-Juvayní to cast away a sum equivalent in value in silver and gold; and impelled those same companions to disdain, and refuse even to touch, the costly furnishings and the coffers of gold and silver which the demoralized and shame-laden Prince Mihdí-Qulí Mírzá, the commander of the army of Mazindarán and a brother of Muhammad Sháh, had left behind in his headlong flight from his camp. We cannot but esteem the passionate sincerity with which Mullá Husayn pleaded with the Prince, and the formal assurance he gave him, disclaiming, in no uncertain terms, any intention on his part or that of his fellow-disciples of usurping the authority of the Sháh or of subverting the foundations of his state. We cannot but view with contempt the conduct of that arch-villain, the hysterical, the cruel and overbearing Sa'ídu'l-'Ulamá, who, alarmed at the approach of those same companions, flung, in a frenzy of excitement, and before an immense crowd of men and women, his turban to the ground, tore open the neck of his shirt, and, bewailing the plight into which Islám had fallen, implored his congregation to fly to arms and cut down the approaching band. We are struck with wonder as we contemplate the super-human prowess of Mullá Husayn which enabled him, notwithstanding his fragile frame and trembling hand, to slay a treacherous foe who had taken shelter behind a tree, by cleaving with a single stroke of his sword the tree, the man and his musket in twain. We are stirred, moreover, by the scene of the arrival of Bahá'u'lláh at the Fort, and the indefinable joy it imparted to Mullá Husayn, the reverent reception accorded Him by His fellow-disciples, His inspection of the fortifications which they had hurriedly erected for their protection, and the ad-

vice He gave them, which resulted in the miraculous deliverance of Quddús, in his subsequent and close association with the defenders of that Fort, and in his effective participation in the exploits connected with its siege and eventual destruction. We are amazed at the serenity and sagacity of that same Quddús, the confidence he instilled on his arrival, the resourcefulness he displayed, the fervor and gladness with which the besieged listened, at morn and at even-tide, to the voice intoning the verses of his celebrated commentary on the Sád of Samad, to which he had already, while in Sarí, devoted a treatise thrice as voluminous as the Qur'án itself, and which he was now, despite the tumultuous attacks of the enemy and the privations he and his companions were enduring, further elucidating by adding to that interpretation as many verses as he had previously written. We remember with thrilling hearts that memorable encounter when, at the cry "Mount your steeds, O heroes of God!" Mullá Husayn, accompanied by two hundred and two of the beleaguered and sorely-distressed companions, and preceded by Quddús, emerged before daybreak from the Fort, and, raising the shout of "Yá Sáhibu'z-Zamán!", rushed at full charge towards the stronghold of the Prince, and penetrated to his private apartments, only to find that, in his consternation, he had thrown himself from a back window into the moat, and escaped bare-footed, leaving his host confounded and routed. We see relived in poignant memory that last day of Mullá Husayn's earthly life, when, soon after midnight, having performed his ablutions, clothed himself in new garments, and attired his head with the Báb's turban, he mounted his charger, ordered the gate of the Fort to be opened, rode out at the head of three hundred and thirteen of his companions, shouting aloud "Yá Sáhibu'z-Zamán!", charged successively the seven barricades erected by the enemy, captured every one of them, notwithstanding the bullets that were raining upon him, swiftly dispatched their defenders, and had scattered their forces when, in the ensuing tumult, his steed became suddenly entangled in the rope of a tent, and before he could extricate himself he was struck in the breast by a bullet which the cowardly 'Abbás-Qulí Khán-i-Laríjaní had discharged, while lying in ambush in the branches of a neighboring tree. We acclaim the magnificent courage that, in a subsequent encounter, inspired nineteen of those stout-hearted companions to plunge headlong into the camp of an enemy that consisted of no less than two regiments of infantry and cavalry, and to cause such consternation that one of their leaders, the same Abbás-Qulí Khán, falling from his horse, and leaving in his distress one of his boots hanging from the stirrup, ran away, half-shod and bewildered, to the Prince, and confessed the ignominious reverse he had suffered. Nor can we fail to note the superb fortitude with which these heroic souls bore the load of their severe trials; when their food was at first reduced to the flesh of horses brought away from the deserted camp of the enemy; when later they had

to content themselves with such grass as they could snatch from the fields whenever they obtained a respite from their besiegers; when they were forced, at a later stage, to consume the bark of the trees and the leather of their saddles, of their belts, of their scabbards and of their shoes; when during eighteen days they had nothing but water of which they drank a mouthful every morning; when the cannon fire of the enemy compelled them to dig subterranean passages within the Fort, where, dwelling amid mud and water, with garments rotting away with damp, they had to subsist on ground up bones; and when, at last, oppressed by gnawing hunger, they, as attested by a contemporary chronicler, were driven to disinter the steed of their venerated leader, Mullá Husayn, cut it into pieces, grind into dust its bones, mix it with the putrified meat, and, making it into a stew, avidly devour it.

Nor can reference be omitted to the abject treachery to which the impotent and discredited Prince eventually resorted, and his violation of his so-called irrevocable oath, inscribed and sealed by him on the margin of the opening Súrah of the Qur'án, whereby he, swearing by that holy Book, undertook to set free all the defenders of the Fort, pledged his honor that no man in his army or in the neighborhood would molest them, and that he would himself, at his own expense, arrange for their safe departure to their homes. And lastly, we call to remembrance, the final scene of that sombre tragedy, when, as a result of the Prince's violation of his sacred engagement, a number of the betrayed companions of Quddús were assembled in the camp of the enemy, were stripped of their possessions, and sold as slaves, the rest being either killed by the spears and swords of the officers, or torn asunder, or bound to trees and riddled with bullets, or blown from the mouths of cannon and consigned to the flames, or else being disemboweled and having their heads impaled on spears and lances. Quddús, their beloved leader, was by yet another shameful act of the intimidated Prince surrendered into the hands of the diabolical Sa'ídu'l-'Ulamá who, in his unquenchable hostility and aided by the mob whose passions he had sedulously inflamed, stripped his victim of his garments, loaded him with chains, paraded him through the streets of Barfurúsh, and incited the scum of its female inhabitants to execrate and spit upon him, assail him with knives and axes, mutilate his body, and throw the tattered fragments into a fire.[39]

THOSE WHO QUAFFED THE CUP OF MARTYRDOM AT FORT SHAYKH TABARSÍ[40] *An excerpt from* ***The Dawn-Breakers***

1. First and foremost among them stands Quddús, upon whom the Báb bestowed the name of Ismu'lláhu'l-Akhar. He, the Last Letter of the Living and the Báb's chosen companion on His pilgrimage to Mecca and Medina, was, together

.with Mullá Sádiq and Mullá Ali-Akbar-i-Ardistani, the first to suffer persecution on Persian soil for the sake of the Cause of God. He was only eighteen years of age when he left his native town of Barfurúsh for Karbilá. For about four years he sat at the feet of Siyyid Kázim, and at the age of twenty-two met and recognised his Beloved in Shíráz. Five years later, on the twenty-third day of Jamádiyu'th-Thání in the year 1265 A.H., he was destined to fall, in the Sabzih-Maydán of Barfurúsh, a victim of the most refined and wanton barbarity at the hands of the enemy. The Báb and, at a later time, Bahá'u'lláh have mourned in unnumbered Tablets and prayers his loss, and have lavished on him their eulogies. Such was the honour accorded to him by Bahá'u'lláh that in His commentary on the verse of Kullu't-Ta'ám, which He revealed while in Baghdád, He conferred upon him the unrivalled station of the Nuqtiy-i-Ukhrá, a station second to none except that of the Báb Himself.

2. Mullá Husayn, surnamed the Bábu'l-Báb, the first to recognise and embrace the new Revelation. At the age of eighteen, he, too, departed from his native town of Bushrúyih in Khurásán for Karbilá, and for a period of nine years remained closely associated with Siyyid Kázim. Four years prior to the Declaration of the Báb, acting according to the instructions of Siyyid Kázim, he met in Isfahán the learned mujtahid Siyyid Báqir-i-Rashtí and in Mashhad Mírzá Askarí, to both of whom he delivered with dignity and eloquence the messages with which he had been entrusted by his leader. The circumstances attending his martyrdom evoked the Báb's inexpressible sorrow, a sorrow that found vent in eulogies and prayers of such great number as would be equivalent to thrice the volume of the Qur'án. In one of His visiting Tablets, the Báb asserts that the very dust of the ground where the remains of Mullá Husayn lie buried is endowed with such potency as to bring joy to the disconsolate and healing to the sick. In the Kitáb-i-Iqán, Bahá'u'lláh extols with still greater force the virtues of Mullá Husayn. "But for him," He writes, "God would not have been established upon the seat of His mercy, nor have ascended the throne of eternal glory!"

3. Mírzá Muhammad-Hasan, the brother of Mullá Husayn.

4. Mírzá Muhammad-Báqir, the nephew of Mullá Husayn. He, as well as Mírzá Muhammad-Hasan, accompanied Mullá Husayn from Bushrúyih to Karbilá and from thence to Shíráz, where they embraced the Message of the Báb and were enrolled among the Letters of the Living. With the exception of the journey of Mullá Husayn to the castle of Máh-Kú, they continued to be with him until the time they suffered martyrdom in the fort of Tabarsí.

5. The brother-in-law of Mullá Husayn, the father of Mírzá Abu'l-Hasan and Mírzá Muhammad-Husayn, both of whom are now in Bushrúyih, and into whose hands the care of the Varaqatu'l-Firdaws, Mullá Husayn's sister, is committed. Both are firm and devoted adherents of the Faith.

6. The son of Mullá Ahmad, the elder brother of Mullá Mírzá Muhammad-i-Furúghí. He, unlike his uncle, Mullá Mírzá Muhammad, suffered martyrdom and was, as testified by the latter, a youth of great piety and distinguished for his learning and his integrity of character.

7. Mírzá Muhammad-Báqir, known as Harátí, though originally a resident of Qá'in. He was a close relative of the father of Nabíl-i-Akbar, and was the first in Mashhad to embrace the Cause. It was he who built the Bábíyyih, and who devotedly served Quddús during his sojourn in that city. When Mullá Husayn hoisted the Black Standard, he, together with his child, Mírzá Muhammad-Kázim, eagerly enrolled under his banner and went forth with him to Mázindarán. That child was saved eventually, and has now grown up into a fervent and active supporter of the Faith in Mashhad. It was Mírzá Muhammad-Báqir who acted as the standard-bearer of the company, who designed the plan of the fort, its walls and turrets and the moat which surrounded it, who succeeded Mullá Husayn in organising the forces of his companions and in leading the charge against the enemy, and who acted as the intimate companion, the lieutenant and trusted counsellor of Quddús until the hour when he fell a martyr in the path of the Cause.

8. Mírzá Muhammad-Taqíy-i-Juvayní, a native of Sabzihvár, who was distinguished for his literary accomplishments and was often entrusted by Mullá Husayn with the task of leading the charge against the assailants. His head and that of his fellow-companion, Mírzá Muhammad-Báqir, were impaled on spears and paraded through the streets of Bárfurúsh, amid the shouts and howling of an excited populace.

9. Qambar-'Alí, the fearless and faithful servant of Mullá Husayn, who accompanied him on his journey to Máh-Kú and who suffered martyrdom on the very night on which his master fell a victim to the bullets of the enemy.

10. Hasan and

11. Qulí, who, together with a man named Iskandar, a native of Zanján, bore the body of Mullá Husayn to the fort on the night of his martyrdom and placed it at the feet of Quddús. He it was, the same Hasan, who, by the orders of the chief constable of Mashhad, was led by a halter through the streets of that city.

12. Muhammad-Hasan, the brother of Mullá Sádiq, whom the comrades of Khusraw slew on the way between Barfurúsh and the fort of Tabarsí. He distinguished himself by his unwavering constancy, and had been one of the servants of the shrine of the Imám Ridá.

13. Siyyid Ridá, who, with Mullá Yúsuf-i-Ardibílí, was commissioned by Quddús to meet the prince, and who brought back with him the sealed copy of the Qur'án bearing the oath which the prince had written. He was one of the well-known siyyids of Khurásán, and was recognised for his learning as well as for the integrity of his character.

14. Mullá Mardán-'Alí, one of the noted companions from Khurásán, a resident of the village of Miyamay, the site of a well-fortified fortress situated between Sabzihvár and Sháh-Rúd. He, together with thirty-three companions, enlisted under the banner of Mullá Husayn on the day of the latter's passage through that village. It was in the masjid of Miyámay, to which Mullá Husayn had repaired in order to offer the Friday congregational prayer, that he delivered his soul-stirring appeal in which he laid stress upon the fulfilment of the tradition relating to the hoisting of the Black Standard in Khurásán, and in which he declared himself to be its bearer. His eloquent address profoundly impressed his hearers, so much so that on that very day the majority of those who heard him, most of whom were men of distinguished merit, arose and followed him. Only one of those thirty-three companions, a Mullá Ísá, survived, whose sons are at present in the village of Miyámay, actively engaged in the service of the Cause. The names of the martyred companions of that village are as follows:

15. Mullá Muhammad-Mihdí,
16. Mullá Muhammad-Ja'far,
17. Mullá Muhammad-ibn-i-Mullá Muhammad,
18. Mullá Rahím,
19. Mullá Muhammad-Ridá,
20. Mullá Muhammad-Husayn,
21. Mullá Muhammad,
22. Mullá Yúsuf,
23. Mullá Ya'qub,
24. Mullá 'Alí,
25. Mullá Zaynu'l-Ábidín,

26. Mullá Muhammad, son of Mullá Zaynu'l-Ábidín,
27. Mullá Báqir,
28. Mullá 'Abdu'l-Muhammad,
29. Mullá Abu'l-Hasan,
30. Mullá Ismá'íl,
31. Mullá Abdu'l-'Alí,
32. Mullá Áqá-Bábá,
33. Mullá 'Abdu'l-Javád,
34. Mullá Muhammad-Husayn,
35. Mullá Muhammad-Báqir,
36. Mullá Muhammad,
37. Hájí Hasan,
38. Kárbilá'í 'Alí,
39. Mullá Kárbilá'í 'Alí,
40. Kárbilá'í Núr-Muhammad,
41. Muhammad-Ibráhím,
42. Muhammad-Sá'im,
43. Muhammad-Hádí,
44. Siyyid Mihdí,
45. Abú-Muhammad.

Of the companions of the village of Sang-Sar, which forms part of the district of Simnán, eighteen were martyred. Their names are as follows:

46. Siyyid Ahmad, whose body was cut to pieces by Mírzá Muhammad-Taqí and the seven 'ulamás of Sárí. He was a noted divine and greatly esteemed for his eloquence and piety.
47. Mír Abu'l-Qásim, Siyyid Ahmad's brother, who won the crown of martyrdom on the very night on which Mullá Husayn met his death.
48. Mír Mihdí, the paternal uncle of Siyyid Ahmad,
49. Mír Ibráhím, the brother-in-law of Siyyid Ahmad,

50. Safar-'Alí, the son of Karbilá'í 'Alí, who, together with Karbilá'í Muhammad, had so strenuously endeavoured to awaken the people of Sang-Sar from their sleep of heedlessness. Both of them, owing to their infirmities, were unable to proceed to the fort of Tabarsí.

51. Muhammad-'Alí, the son of Karbilá'í Abú-Muhammad,

52. Abu'l-Qásim, the brother of Muhammad-'Alí,

53. Kárbilá'í Ibráhím,

54. 'Alí-Ahmad,

55. Mullá 'Alí-Akbar,

56. Mullá Husayn-'Alí,

57. 'Abbás-'Alí,

58. Husayn-'Alí,

59. Mullá 'Alí-Asghar,

60. Karbilá'í Ismá'íl,

61. 'Alí Khán,

62. Muhammad-Ibráhím,

63. 'Abdu'l-'Azím.

From the village of Shah-Mírzád, two fell in defending the fort:

64. Mullá Abú-Rahím and

65. Karbilá'í Kázim.

As to the adherents of the Faith in Mázindarán, twenty-seven martyrs have thus far been recorded:

66. Mullá Riday-i-Sháh,

67. 'Azím,

68. Karbilá'í Muhammad-Ja'far,

69. Siyyid Husayn,

70. Muhammad-Báqir,

71. Siyyid Razzáq,

72. Ustád Ibráhím,

73. Mullá Sa'íd-i-Zirih-Kinárí,

74. Ridáy-i-'Arab,
75. Rasúl-i-Bahnimírí,
76. Muhammad-Husayn, the brother of Rasúl-i-Bahnimírí,
77. Táhir,
78. Shafí',
79. Qásim,
80. Mullá Muhammad-Ján,
81. Masíh, the brother of Mullá Muhammad-Ján,
82. Itá-Bábá,
83. Yúsuf,
84. Fadlu'lláh,
85. Bábá,
86. Safí-Qulí,
87. Nizám,
88. Rúhu'lláh,
89. 'Alí-Qulí,
90. Sultán,
91. Ja'far,
92. Khalíl.

Of the believers of Savád-Kúh, the five following names have thus far been ascertained:

93. Karbilá'í Qambar-Kálish,
94. Mullá Nád-'Alíy-i-Mutavallí,
95. Abdu'l-Haqq,
96. Itábakí-Chúpán,
97. Son of Itábakí-Chúpán.

From the town of Ardistán, the following have suffered martyrdom:

98. Mírzá 'Alí-Muhammad, son of Mírzá Muhammad-Sa'íd,
99. Mírzá Abdu'l-Vási', son of Hájí Abdu'l-Vahháb,

100. Muhammad-Husayn, son of Hájí Muhammad-Sádiq,

101. Muhammad-Mihdí, son of Hájí Muhammad-Ibráhím,

102. Mírzá Ahmad, son of Muhsin,

103. Mírzá Muhammad, son of Mír Muhammad-Taqí.

From the city of Isfahán, thirty have thus far been recorded:

104. Mullá Ja'far, the sifter of wheat, whose name has been mentioned by the Báb in the Persian Bayán.

105. Ustád Áqá, surnamed Buzurg-Banná,

106. Ustád Hasan, son of Ustád Áqá,

107. Ustád Muhammad, son of Ustád Áqá,

108. Muhammad-Husayn, son of Ustád Áqá, whose younger brother Ustád Ja'far was sold several times by his enemies until he reached his native city, where he now resides.

109. Ustád Qurbán-'Alíy-i-Banná,

110. 'Alí-Akbar, son of Ustád Qurbán-'Alíy-i-Banná,

111. 'Abdu'lláh, son of Ustád Qurbán-'Alíy-i-Banná,

112. Muhammad-i-Báqir-Naqsh, the maternal uncle of Siyyid Yahyá, son of Mírzá Muhammad-'Alíy-i-Nahrí. He was fourteen years old and was martyred the very night that Mullá Husayn met his death.

113. Mullá Muhammad-Taqí,

114. Mullá Muhammad-Ridá, both brothers of the late Abdu's-Sálih, the gardener of the Ridván at Akká.

115. Mullá Ahmad-i-Saffár,

116. Mullá Husayn-i-Miskar,

117. Ahmad-i-Payvandí,

118. Hasan-i-Sha'r-Báf-i-Yazdí,

119. Muhammad-Taqí,

120. Muhammad-'Attár, brother of Hasan-i-Sha'r-Báf,

121. Mullá Abdu'l-Kháliq, who cut his throat in Badasht and whom Táhirih named Dhabíh.

122. Husayn,

123. Abu'l-Qásim, brother of Husayn,
124. Mírzá Muhammad-Ridá,
125. Mullá Haydar, brother of Mírzá Muhammad-Ridá,
126. Mírzá Mihdí,
127. Muhammad-Ibráhím,
128. Muhammad-Husayn, surnamed Dastmál-Girih-Zan,
129. Muhammad-Hasan-i-Chít-Sáz, a well-known cloth manufacturer who attained the presence of the Báb.
130. Muhammad-Husayn-i-'Attár,
131. Ustád Hájí Muhammad-i-Banná,
132. Mahmúd-i-Muqári'í, a noted cloth dealer. He was newly married and had attained the presence of the Báb in the castle of Chihríq. The Báb urged him to proceed to the Jazíriy-i-Khadrá and to lend his assistance to Quddús. While in Tihrán, he received a letter from his brother announcing the birth of a son and entreating him to hasten to Isfahán to see him, and then to proceed to whichever place he felt inclined. "I am too much fired," he replied, "with the love of this Cause to be able to devote any attention to my son. I am impatient to join Quddús and to enlist under his banner."
133. Siyyid Muhammad-Ridáy-i-Pá-Qal'iyí, a distinguished siyyid and a highly esteemed divine, whose declared purpose to enlist under the banner of Mullá Husayn caused a great tumult among the 'ulamás of Isfahán.

Among the believers of Shíráz, the following attained the station of martyrdom:

134. Mullá 'Abdu'lláh, known also by the name of Mírzá Sálih,
135. Mullá Zaynu'l-'Ábidín,
136. Mírzá Muhammad.

Of the adherents of the Faith in Yazd, only four have thus far been recorded:

137. The siyyid who walked on foot all the way from Khurásán to Bárfurúsh, where he fell a victim to the bullet of the enemy.
138. Siyyid Ahmad, the father of Siyyid Husayn-i-'Azíz, the amanuensis of the Báb,
139. Mírzá Muhammad-'Alí, son of Siyyid Ahmad, whose head was blown off by the ball from a cannon as he was standing at the entrance of the fort, and who, because of his tender age, was greatly loved and admired by Quddús.

140. Shaykh 'Alí, son of Shaykh 'Abdu'l-Kháliq-i-Yazdí, a resident of Mashhad, a youth whose enthusiasm and untiring energy were greatly praised by Mullá Husayn and Quddús.

Of the believers of Qazvín, the following were martyred:

141. Mírzá Muhammad-'Alí, a noted divine, whose father, Hájí Mullá Abdu'l-Vahháb, was one of the most distinguished mujtahids in Qazvín. He attained the presence of the Báb in Shíráz, and was enrolled as one of the Letters of the Living.

142. Muhammad-Hádí, a noted merchant, son of Hájí 'Abdu'l-Karím, surnamed Bághbán-Báshí,

143. Siyyid Ahmad,

144. Mírzá Abdu'l-Jalíl, a noted divine,

145. Mírzá Mihdí.

146. From the village of Lahárd, a man named Hájí Muhammad-'Alí, who had greatly suffered as a result of the murder of Mullá Taqí in Qazvín.

Of the believers of Khuy, the following have suffered martyrdom:

147. Mullá Mihdí, a distinguished divine, who had been one of the esteemed disciples of Siyyid Kázim. He was noted for his learning, his eloquence, and his staunchness of faith.

148. Mullá Mahmúd-i-Khu'í, brother of Mullá Mihdí, one of the Letters of the Living and a distinguished divine.

149. Mullá Yúsuf-i-Ardibílí, one of the Letters of the Living, noted for his learning, his enthusiasm and eloquence. It was he who had aroused the apprehensions of Hájí Karím Khán on his arrival at Kirmán, and who struck terror to the hearts of his adversaries. "This man," Hájí Karím Khán was heard to say to his congregation, "must needs be expelled from this town, for if he be allowed to remain, he will assuredly cause the same tumult in Kirmán as he has already done in Shíráz. The injury he will inflict will be irreparable. The magic of his eloquence and the force of his personality, if they do not already excel those of Mullá Husayn, are certainly not inferior to them." By this means he was able to force him to curtail his stay in Kirmán and to prevent him from addressing the people from the pulpit. The Báb gave him the following instructions: "You must visit the towns and cities of Persia and summon their inhabitants to the Cause of God. On the first day of the month of Muharram in the

year 1265 A.H. (27 November 1845 A.D.), you must be in Mázindarán and must arise to lend every assistance in your power to Quddús." Mullá Yúsuf, faithful to the instructions of his Master, refused to prolong his stay beyond a week in any of the towns and cities which he visited. On his arrival in Mázindarán, he was made captive by the forces of Prince Mihdí-Qulí Mírzá, who immediately recognised him and gave orders that he be imprisoned. He was eventually released, as we have already observed, by the companions of Mullá Husayn on the day of the battle of Vás-Kas.

150. Mullá Jalíl-i-Urúmí, one of the Letters of the Living, noted for his learning, his eloquence, and tenacity of faith.

151. Mullá Ahmad, a resident of Marághih, one of the Letters of the Living, and a distinguished disciple of Siyyid Kázim.

152. Mullá Mihdíy-i-Kandí, a close companion of Bahá'u'lláh, and a tutor to the children of His household.

153. Mullá Báqir, brother of Mullá Mihdí, both of whom were men of considerable learning, to whose great attainments Bahá'u'lláh testifies in the "Kitáb-i-Íqán."

154. Siyyid Kázim, a resident of Zanján, and one of its noted merchants. He attained the presence of the Báb in Shíráz, and accompanied Him to Isfahán. His brother, Siyyid Murtadá, was one of the Seven Martyrs of Tihrán.

155. Iskandar, also a resident of Zanján, who, together with Hasan and Qulí, bore the body of Mullá Husayn to the fort.

156. Ismá'íl,

157. Karbilá'í 'Abdu'l-'Alí,

158. 'Abdu'l-Muhammad,

159. Hájí 'Abbás,

160. Siyyid Ahmad--all residents of Zanján.

161. Siyyid Husayn-i-Kuláh-Dúz, a resident of Bárfurúsh, whose head was impaled on a lance and was paraded through its streets.

162. Mullá Hasan-i-Rashtí,

163. Mullá Hasan-i-Bayájmandí,

164. Mullá Ni'matu'lláh-i-Bárfurúshí,

165. Mullá Muhammad-Taqíy-i-Qarákhílí,

166. Ustád Zaynu'l-'Ábidín,

167. Ustád Qásim, son of Ustád Zaynu'l-Ábidín,

168. Ustád 'Alí-Akbar, brother of Ustád Zaynu'l-Ábidín.

The last three were masons by profession, were natives of Kirmán, and resided in Qáyin in the province of Khurásán.

169 and 170. Mullá Ridáy-i-Sháh and a young man from Bahnimír were slain two days after the abandonment of the fort by Quddús, in the Panj-Shanbih-Bázár of Bárfurúsh. Hájí Mullá Muhammad-i-Hamzih, surnamed the Sharí'at-Madár, succeeded in burying their bodies in the neighbourhood of the Masjid-i-Kázim-Big, and in inducing their murderer to repent and ask forgiveness.

171. Mullá Muhammad-i-Mu'allim-i-Núrí, an intimate companion of Bahá'u'lláh who was closely associated with Him in Núr, in Tihrán, and in Mázindarán. He was famed for his intelligence and learning, and was subjected, Quddús only excepted, to the severest atrocities that have ever befallen a defender of the fort of Tabarsí. The prince had promised that he would release him on condition that he would execrate the name of Quddús, and had pledged his word that, should he be willing to recant, he would take him back with him to Tihrán and make him the tutor of his sons. "Never will I consent," he replied, "to vilify the beloved of God at the bidding of a man such as you. Were you to confer upon me the whole of the kingdom of Persia, I would not for one moment turn my face from my beloved leader. My body is at your mercy, my soul you are powerless to subdue. Torture me as you will, that I may be enabled to demonstrate to you the truth of the verse, 'Then, wish for death, if ye be men of truth.'" The prince, infuriated by his answer, gave orders that his body be cut to pieces and that no effort be spared to inflict upon him a most humiliating punishment.

172. Hájí Muhammad-i-Karrádí, whose home was situated in one of the palm groves adjoining the old city of Baghdád, a man of great courage who had fought and led a hundred men in the war against Ibráhím Páshá of Egypt. He had been a fervent disciple of Siyyid Kázim, and was the author of a long poem in which he expatiated upon the virtues and merits of the siyyid. He was seventy-five years old when he embraced the Faith of the Báb, whom he likewise eulogised in an eloquent and detailed poem. He distinguished himself by his heroic acts during the siege of the fort, and eventually became a victim of the bullets of the enemy.

173. Sa'íd-i-Jabbáví, a native of Baghdád, who displayed extraordinary courage during the siege. He was shot in the abdomen, and, though severely wounded,

managed to walk until he reached the presence of Quddús. He joyously threw himself at his feet and expired.

The circumstances of the martyrdom of these last two companions were related by Siyyid Abú-Tálib-i-Sang-Sará, one of those who survived that memorable siege, in a communication he addressed to Bahá'u'lláh. In it he relates, in addition, his own story, as well as that of his two brothers, Siyyid Ahmad and Mír Abú'l-Qásim, both of whom were martyred while defending the fort. "On the day on which Khusraw was slain," he wrote, "I happened to be the guest of a certain Karbilá'í 'Alí-Ján, the kad-khudá of one of the villages in the neighbourhood of the fort. He had gone to assist in the protection of Khusraw, and had returned and was relating to me the circumstances attending his death. On that very day, a messenger informed me that two Arabs had arrived at that village and were anxious to join the occupants of the fort. They expressed their fear of the people of the village of Qádí-Kalá, and promised that they would amply reward whoever would be willing to conduct them to their destination. I recalled the counsels of my father, Mír Muhammad-'Alí, who exhorted me to arise and help in the promotion of the Cause of the Báb. I immediately decided to seize the opportunity that had presented itself to me, and, together with these two Arabs, and with the aid and assistance of the Kad-khudá, reached the fort, met Mullá Husayn, and determined to consecrate the remaining days of my life to the service of the Cause he had chosen to follow."

(1) God is Calling You From this World[41]
by Na'ím

O seeker of God, God is calling you –
His Holiness, the Glorious One is calling you.

The Eternal Essence is beckoning you
from the mortal world to the eternal realm.

O thou who art waiting and eager, hasten!
God is calling you to the festive reunion!

O thou earthly one, since He summons you from the nether world
to the heavenly abode, become celestial!

In the midst of war and strife, the Incomparable God
beckons you toward peace and delight.

His servants are drawn into the sea of destruction.
He is calling on you for sacrifice.

O thou darvísh sitting on the roadside, the true King
is beckoning you to the rank of the prophets!

He is calling you to the Most Great Peace,
to the welfare of humankind, to the religion of Bahá.

Establishing the unity of all who dwell on earth[42]
is an obligation of all the people of conscience.

(2) From Varqá with Love[43]
by Varqá (martyred)

If thou art a wayfarer, O thou treading the path,
become an ensign in the path of love,
overcome all traces of self,
become unsurpassed in intellect and reason.

O thou illuminated essence,
O thou exalted by human attributes,
die to the world of animal passions
and become a true human being,

for you are the essence of "I" and "We."
In you are all the names and attributes.
You are both the sun and the sea;
therefore, bestir yourself and manifest your light!

Be aware that you are intoxicated,
that you are ignorant of "Am I not. . .?"[44]
If you are a Friend-worshiper,
become both a pilgrim and a gnostic.[45]

Be not afraid of God's Bounty!
By knowing God, know thine own self![46]
O spirit of God amongst His people,
Be like Jesus, Son of Mary.

If you be of the people of the heart, say, "Yá Hú!"[47]
Search out one who has the breath of spirit;[48]
become a companion and a wayfaring friend
to the one who is sincere of heart.

O behold the majesty of the King!
Observe the divine mysteries!
Behold the Spirit reveling
and become yourself light incarnate!

Associate with the pure ones.
Behold the lights of truth.
Become steadfast and strong
in the verities of science and religion.

Attain the station of love and affection.
Be among those who befriend.
Go enter the realms of paradise.
Abandon the province of hell.

Approach the dawning place of victory
and drink a cup of divine assistance
that you might become a lamp in the dark night
and a sea of benevolence on the dry land.

I have concealed these secrets in this pearl[49]
and have foregone the clamor of fame
that you might become
enlightened by this breath.[50]

Become the first and the last.
Become the manifest and the hidden.
Become the revealer and the concealer.
Become the beginning and the seal.[51]

Drink deep from the cup of Unity.
Put on the garment of eternity.
Strive to acquire the divine science
that thou mayest be a true and learned scholar.

Behold the eloquence of that silent one.
Behold the refinement of his admonitions.
Hearken to that splendid music.
Become tranquil and carefree.

In the garment of nudity
there exists a hidden mystery.
Become the revered master –
What do you really know about us?

If you imbibe but a sip of Truth,
you would close your eyes to all else.
O particle of dust, why do you wander about?
O thou drop, become now a sea!

Seek not ascendancy over others.
That dart will then become but an aperitif.
How long will you strive for increase?
Become abundant but insignificant! [52]

The Intended One is addressing you!
Hurry! He is speaking!
Listen! Hear what He is saying!
"Arise and be resolute!"

Let your self become absorbed by gazing on Him!
Become enamored with the light of His glory!
Become entangled in the midst
of His jet black hair!

Enter this garden with us!
Join the drunken ones!
Take this goblet from us that
by Jam's cup you can behold the universe.[53]

From the dark night did the morn dawn,
and the days did thus become illumined by Him.
O Star, hovering in our heavens,
Go! Become the Great Sun!

Transcend this stage of existence!
Hearken to the bird of steadfastness!
If thou art a wayfarer, O thou treading the path,
Become an ensign in the path of love!

(3) FROM THE MATHNAVÍ ANVARÍYYIH[54]
BY VARQÁ (MARTYRED)

O Thou who has caused all the Prophets to be in wonderment
and the saints to be dumbstruck with amazement,

a hundred thousand sanctified souls and pure spirits
have cast their undefiled lives on the earth in Your path.

A hundred thousand Adams in Your quarter
are saying to You, "O Lord, we have wronged ourselves."[55]

A hundred thousand drawn like the savior Noah
into the storm seek refuge in Your benevolence.

A hundred thousand like the burnt Khalíl[56]
have walked into the blazoning fire

until they have become sanctified from all impurities;
the crucible of love has transformed the fire into a flower garden.[57]

A hundred thousand like the brave Ishmael
Have sacrificed themselves for You because of their affection.

A hundred thousand like Kalím[58]
have swooned before Your light.

A hundred thousand like the patient Ayyúb[59]
Have become thankful servants in the midst of Your calamity.

A hundred thousand in this world have, like Jesus,
given their lives on the gallows of Your friendship.

A hundred thousand servants in Your path have,
like Muhammad ascending, attained Your Mi'ráj.[60]

A hundred thousand saints, pure and sanctified spirits,
have shed their blood on the earth in Your path.

A hundred thousand have been slain for Your friendship,
like Husayn in the sands of Karbilá.

Throughout the land there is not one particle of soil
that has not been drenched with undefiled blood.

Because of separation from You, many seas
and streams and springs have flowed from eyes.

Anywhere a fire is kindled or a lightning bolt
has burned a heap of wheat,

it is but the spark from the breast of a mystic[61]
or a flame from the path of a seeker's heart.

On the path of Your eager ones, O Thou with attributes of Abhá,
these gusting winds are blowing.

The shining of the sun is caused by Your conflagration;
The redness of the world is from Your bloodshed.

From the fire of Your love, O King of Hearts,
the life and soul of both man and jinnee are consumed.[62]

There is no heart that is not feverish in Your path;
there is no eye that is not crying in longing for You.

Anywhere there exists a heart, it is heavy with blood because of You;[63]
anywhere there exists a mind, it is perplexed, bewildered because of You.

(4) THE LOVER'S ABLUTION[64]
BY VARQÁ (MARTYRED)

Although murder is sinful
for those with learning and wisdom,
for an assassin like You
to take my life is perfectly lawful.

For while there is no one in this world
eager for his own drowning,
I have no desire for the shore
here in the depths of the ocean of Your love.

Cannot my admonishing friends see
that my eyes are fixed on His face?
O my counselors, for the sake of God,
cease these idle cautions.

What? Did you think my obligatory prayer
was lacking proper ablutions?
Did you not know that the lover's ablution
is incomplete without the heart's blood?[65]

I hearkened unto the arch of Your brow
and became entangled in Your jet black hair;[66]
I know not whether to call You the Praiseworthy One,
or simply He who is Just.[67]

With Your fathomless elegance and beauty
You are the destroyer of the gnostic lover;
With the plentitude of Your heavenly virtues,
You are the object of every pious scholar's quest.

O those of you who are insane with love,
since the pious ones are ignorant of the ecstacy
of your love for the Beloved of Hearts,
conceal if you can the secrets of your heart.

Since that moment when I placed
my aching love for You in my heart,
there is no longer any room there
for the sorrows of this world.

O Beloved, I have nothing fitting
to offer at Your feet,
except this meager token of my life,
an unworthy gift for You.

There is no leaven for the friends
except reunion with Him.
O my heart, if you desire true life,
never forget that truth.

There are so many songs of love for You
that overflow from Varqá's love-sick heart,
that were he for even a moment to part his lips,
they would burn to ashes this body of water and clay.

(5) THE GARDEN OF LOVE[68]
BY 'USTÁD MUHAMMAD 'ALÍ SALMÁNÍ

In the flower-laden garden,
when would a nightingale
that has nested there a lifetime
neglect the blossom to study the thorn?

At times he weeps, at times he laughs,
at times he warbles, at times he laments,
but once in wonder, singing lyric tunes,
his gaze is solely on the Beloved.

Once drawn into the sea of His love,
the lover heeds not the shore;
his soul, longing for the tumult
of thrashing waves, disdains safe harbor.

Solely the seller of lives has a booth
in the joyous bazaar of His love;
how could the selfish, the brutish,
or the unrefined expect a place here?

When does one gazing at the sun
ever give heed to the darkness?
When does one enthralled with the Friend
ever heed the stranger's presence?

The one who treads Your path
would cleanse his hands and heart of life.
The one who associates with You
seeks naught save Your good pleasure.

Such a wondrous and mystic clime
envelops this mystic garden –
soil of fire, blossoms of fire,
fire pouring forth from clouds above.

Is it the pen of 'Abdu'l-Bahá,
or Khidr returned from the darkness,[69]
like a bird that has the "water of life"
flowing from its beak?

Any heart possessed by the love of Bahá
can not simultaneously be in love with the world
any more than a royal falcon
would scavenge a dead corpse.

(6) Mazi Dárad[70]
by Liqá'í Káshání

The disheveled ringlet on your
moonlike face is heavenly!
The hyacinth winding around
the flower is delightful!

My soul is on my lips.[71]
Why doesn't the Friend enter in?
My lip on the Beloved's lip
would be delightful!

How strange, how very strange –
such vain imagining, impossible desires:
a mere darvísh at the King's feast.
It would be delightful!

I have no fear of being slaughtered
in His quarter –
the sacrifice of this lifeless bird
would be delightful!

The tumult of the crowd behind,
the drum and tambour leading the way,
and I, dancing towards the town square,
would be so delightful!

O Shaykh, do not bother me!
Stop warning me about this adoration!
For this love-sick one, the taunting of rivals
is truly delightful!

Do not trouble yourself to offer
a sermon or useless admonitions.
The fire burning in my soul
is simply delightful!

O Liqá'í, since we are drowned
in the sea of nothingness,
warning us about the severity of rain
would be delightful!

(7) He is the Intended One[72]
by Rúhu'lláh[73] (martyred)

O Cupbearer, fill my cup to the brim!
Fill my heart's túr with the fire of Your wine!

Bestow a goblet of the wine of "Am I not. . .?"
that I may awaken from intoxicated sleep,

that I may rend the veils of fancies and vain imaginings,
that I may ascend to the zenith of the seventh heaven,

that I may escape the dark snare of water and clay,
that I may take my flight to the sanctified kingdom,

that I may free myself from this realm of toil and tests,
that I may turn my face towards the native land of my soul

and inhale from that garden of the spirit the fragrance of the Friend
then return like breezes blowing from the abode of the Friend

accompanied by a fragrant, life-giving breath to bespeak
those blessed glad tidings that remove all sorrow,

to proclaim brazenly to the friends in every region:
"Hasten, O friends, for this is the Day of the Covenant!

"Hasten, O lovers of the face of the Friend!
With sincere hearts turn your gaze toward the abode of the Friend!

"O companions, treasure this propitious moment, so precious,
so unique that you might assist and uphold the Cause of God!

"O friends, strive ye that this immaculate Faith
might be spread throughout the entire globe.

"O friends, exert yourselves that the Word of the Omnipotent Lord
might become recognized and honored throughout the earth,

"that the drunken ones may become conscious
and may abandon idle fancies and vain imaginings,

"that their eyes may become brightened by the light of God
and the thicket of their hearts transmuted into a garden of flowers.

"O friends, now indeed is the time, the time of service,
the time for acquiring divine bounty, the time of victory.

"O ye friends of Bahá, turn towards the world
carrying aloft banners of guidance.

"This is that which the King of the Ancient Eternity
commanded the nations in His Kitáb-i-Aqdas:

"'Whosoever arises to serve the Cause of God,
the Lord of Creation will make him victorious.

"'Whosoever sacrifices his life for the Covenant of God,
the face of God Himself will watch over him.'"

O Cupbearer, grant me a cup of your benevolence
that I might become purified from any sin or shortcoming,

for though my sins may be beyond reckoning,
I am filled with hope because of God's forgiveness.

Welcome, O Cupbearer from the Ancient Feast!
Pour but a drop of Thy benevolence on this clay

that by Your bounty flecks of dust may become brilliant suns,
may become worthy of martyrdom before the Beloved.

O God, when will it take place that in Your quarter
I will sacrifice my life for my adoration of Your countenance?

How happy will be the day when in the field of love
I can surrender my life in the path of the Most Beloved of Lovers!

How joyous the moment when upon the gallows
I will brazenly proclaim the praises of the King of Bahá!

O God, when that day finally comes to pass,
I will at last become free from this withered body.

I will face towards the paradise of Eternity!
I will become verdant and fresh through the bounty of nearness!

Behold me now in flames from the fire of separation,
burning in the desert of privation!

O King of my soul, cast off the veil from Your face
that the heavens may become illumined by Your light!

O King of the Covenant! O Monarch of God's Covenant!
O Thou from whose light the Paran[74] of the Covenant is ablaze!

O Thou who hast titled yourself 'Abdu'l-Bahá,[75]
By your command the ensigns of guidance are raised!

You are aware of the dawning place of divine secrets!
You are the source of divine utterance![76]

O powerful King of Kings, you are like alif,[77]
stalwart within the Cause of the Creator,

yet humble like bá in your servitude before the gate[78]
of the shrine[79] of the Lord of Bahá.

O Thou, the Greatest Branch of the Tree of this Cause,
O Thou, "the Branch sprung from the Ancient Root,"[80]

the One who is the dawning place of God's Revelation,
through whom the eyes of the people of Bahá become enlightened,

cast but a drop of benevolence on this mournful bird
which has become impatient and restless in separation from you!

My heart has been set ablaze by the fire of separation from you!
Remoteness from you cast sparks on my water and clay!

O King of the Kingdom of Souls, Help me!
My heart is aflame in its remoteness from you!

O King, I burn in the fire of separation
in this desert of remoteness and fervor.

O King of all benevolence, O Monarch of charity,
rescue this bird from the snare of despondency:

"Look not at my merit or capacity;
Behold, instead, Your own magnanimity, O Thou the Giver!"[81]

(8) Tears of the Dove[82]
by 'Abdí

In the morning when Sabá
was kissing the flowers,
the shadow of a feather and a wing
broke the silence of the meadow;

two doves settled on a branch,
the one with the blossom of love
in its mouth was following
close behind the other.

The butterfly, unconscious
from the sweet lips of the anemone,
and those two light-winged doves,
drunk in the bosom of spring,

made the dew laugh while the flowers
and grass became enraptured.
The meadow itself became revived
from all the kissing and caressing.

For a while in a bridal bower[83]
of eglantine and white jasmine,
they would wash their breasts
with dew from the petals at dawn.

Then, in a pool of water,
they would thrash their wings
or search for seeds amid the mound
of blossoms along the garden path.

At that moment,
the doves talked softly
that they might not fall prey
to the cunning hunter's trap.

Suddenly, from the soil
of a quiet grave along the path,
there arose the scent
of tuberose and jasmine.

One of them hopped
upon that flower-covered grave
and sang, "O my pampered one,
here lies all love and hope!"

The beloved answered,
"Speak softer, O leaven of life."
Then a tear dropped
from her cheek.

"Not every place where flowers
and jasmine bloom is joyful;
this mound of blossoms is the grave
of an unfortunate martyr.

"The tulip has become tinted
red from the martyr's blood,
and the sky is rose-colored
from shedding so many tears."

The swift-winged bird felt
ashamed of his words,[84]
and the tears of his beloved
kindled a fire in his heart.

With bright beams the sun
pitched its tent everywhere
as talk continued
about that heart-singed lover:

"Years ago, after the death
of the depraved king,
a band of infernal spirits
showed their horrid faces!

"Mounted on steeds of anger,
the perverse enemy[85]
went forth in that peril to extinguish
the star of the Varqá of paradise.[86]

"Far from the clamor and mischief
of these detestable ravens,
a father and son sat
bound in burdensome chains.

"But, knowing that God's indomitable
will is ever benign and just,
they happily submitted
their own will to the will of God.

"'O father! What is that clamor?
Do you hear it?
At last the firmament
is pulsating for you this day!'

"'Farewell, my son,' the father
replied to his precious pearl.
'The promised time
has now arrived.'

"Laughter came from the rotted prison door
as in came the fiend warning
that this was no time
for chatting and whispering.

"But that child of love
pulled himself up to his full height:
'No lion cub like me
lingers long in the corner of a cage!'

"The voice of the executioner became calm:
'O walking cypress,[87]
no one could wither you,
fresh blossom that you are.'

"The boy answered, 'There is not one
of the lovers of the Blessed Beauty
who would not anoint his face with ambergris
from the dust of His feet.'

"Like lightning from the clouds,
the dagger of the bloodthirsty Hájib
descended and tore open
the father's side.

"Since the child did not heed
the executioner's advice,
a yoke was fastened to his neck
and firmly bound.

"The burnt moth was saying
to the candle of its existence,
'O my soul, you are relieved
from this suffering and misery.[88]

"'Never did our minds
become happy through good fortune;
we are leaving,
and this fate has been our destiny!'

"The gathering place of the Day of God[89]
appeared that day
as the pure blood of the martyrs
was poured on the pages of history.

"The executioner witnessed
so much cruelty from a ravenous people,
that he was stunned and placed
a finger aside his face in wonder.

"Wailing and lamentation
of children reached the heavens;
mothers followed their sons
to the field of sacrifice.

"The mother of the lion-hearted ones
said in loud voice:
'Let the life of this precious child
be a sacrifice for Bahá!'"[90]

When the tale of the Varqá's heroism
reached this point,
a flock of birds
were flying in the sky.

Both doves flew to the
wheel of the celestial sphere,[91]
where they told this story
to all the other birds:

"My heart blazes
from within the tight cage of my breast,
a fire from whose heat
the rays of the sun appeared.

"It will grow from the drop
of a tear that dropped on this spot,
a red tulip from the grave
of Varqá the martyr."

(9) ALAS! ALAS![92]
BY NAYYIR AND SINÁ

Alas, Alas, O Land of Tá,[93]
what has happened to Varqá? Where is he,[94]
that dove of the garden of Abhá Beauty?
What befell him,

that pheasant of the flower garden of Unity?
Where is he,
that holy gazelle of the Abhá plain?
What happened to him?

O Sabá, O East wind,[95]
where is Varqá's darling son?
Where is that eloquent nightingale
with his beauteous songs?

Where is that youthful, tender shoot,
that elegant effulgent bloom
not yet fully blossomed?
What became of him?

That harmonious Dove[96] with his joyous melodies -
Where is he?
And what befell
the sugar-shedding parrot?

Where is the chick of the Símurgh[97]
of the Qáf of nearness?
Where is the fawn of the deer[98]
of the desert plains of Há?[99]

Where is the exhilarating voice
of Rúhu'lláh?
Where is the awe-inspiring melody
of Varqá?

Without his presence
our gatherings are gloomy.
O Alas! Where is he
who so adorned our assemblage?[100]

If Háhjib thought this slaughter just,
where was the trial held?
Where were the judges?
Where was an authentic decree?[101]

No one knows where lies
his defiled corpse,
or where that luminous ethereal
essence has gone.

If he walked into the fire
as Khalíl did in ages past,[102]
then where is the blossom,
and where the red tulip?

Or if like Jonah
he went into the mouth of a fish,
why did he not escape after
as did Jonah?

Or if like Joseph
he was ripped apart by a wolf,
what happened to the cloak
soaked with false blood?

And if he was not devoured by the wolf
but was thrown into a well,
what happened to the story of the bucket
when the wayfarer said: "Ah there! Good news!"?[103]

And if like John his blood
was poured upon a tray,
where is his head and
where his beauteous body?

And if like Jesus he was
lifted upon a cross,
then where was the tumult of crowds
and the attack of the people?

If his head was severed
like that of Husayn,
where is the pure
and radiant body?

And if by the sword and dagger
he was hacked into pieces,
why does no one ask
"What happened to those limbs?"

As the flute laments its separation,[104]
so Nayyir and Siná lament,
singing, "What has happened
to that faithful friend of ours?"

(10) The Story of Hájí Mullá Hasan [105]
by Nabíl-i-A'zam (Martyred) [106]

One of these was Hasan, an illuminating moon,
whose hair had become like milk from following the path of loyalty.

He possessed piety and knowledge, yoked with resplendent deeds,
perseverance, and, in the face of calamity, the meekness of a lamb.

In a dream on that last night, his beloved Abhá appeared to him
like the illuminating sun and spoke to him these words:

"O Hasan," He said, "without any doubt your name has been entered
in the book of those who have offered up their lives for faith.[107]

"But if you be not content with this fate,
tell me now that I may change your destiny."[108]

"No, by God!" Hasan replied. "Would that I had a hundred souls
that I might gladly sacrifice them all at Your feet!"

The Monarch replied, "O true friend, since you are thus content,
your two fellow prisoners may be also blessed to share your destiny."

As soon as Hasan awakened from this dream,
he shared the promise with his companions.

They both said to him, "This is but vain imaginings!
It is certain that we all shall be freed tomorrow!"

"No, no!" Hasan replied. "Whether or not ye be content,
all three of us will be sacrificed this very day!

"The Beloved Himself has said so! There is no way
to countermand it! Be thou content with His desire!"

An hour had not passed ere from that place
all three were taken to the place of slaughter.

All three gave their lives away – Hasan with felicity.
the other two with great sighing and sorrow.

(11) The Master Builder[109]
by Na'ím

The story of these lovers shall eclipse from our memories
the fable of Majnún and the legend of Farhád,[110]

these lovers who paced to the place of execution
more eagerly than a groom hastening to the bridal chamber.

It is His beauty that hath made slaves of the masters
and freed slaves from their bondage.[111]

One dwelled in sorrow and torture;
the other fell into calamity and suffering.

One set his own household on fire;
another offered up his family to the wind.

This one sacrificed his possessions; that one, his child;
another, his ambition; and another, his own life.

Among so many destroyers, how did the Master Builder
fashion this house so that it flourishes and overflows with friends?

Behold how firm He made the foundation of this Cause,
even amid the tumult – the waves of tests and storms.

The mind is astonished! May His sovereignty be exalted!
And may His station be glorified![112]

(12) Except in this Faith[113]
by Na'ím

Except in this Faith
have you ever heard
of a wise one wishing
to hasten to his own death?

Except in Dáru's-Salám,[114]
have you ever seen anyone
let himself be slaughtered
by his own hand?

Except in Tihrán,
have you ever heard of a sane one
pacing for three months to deliver
a letter ordaining his own execution?[115]

Except in Zanján
have you ever heard of a mother
encouraging the execution
of her own son?[116]

Except in Shíráz,
is there a place where one
eagerly gives a reward
to an ignorant assassin?

Except in Isfahán,
has anyone ever given
blood money to a rabid killer
to expedite his own murder?

Except in 'Ishqábád,
did you ever witness
one who would intercede
on behalf of a murderer?

Except in Yazd,
has anyone ever uttered
such words as these
while being slaughtered:

I desire no helper[117]
to help me,
but I do desire a witness
to watch me.[118]

(13) The Unseen Threads of Destiny[119]
by Muhammad Báháu'd-Dín 'Abdí

That cruel Qájár king, having neither prudence nor foresight,
could not have guessed how this game of destiny would end.

Innocent servants at the hall of the magistrate –
none of them guilty – were condemned at the pleasure of the Sháh.

He tied the Beloved of the world with such a weighty chain
that heaven itself could not endure its loathsome links.

He whose heart is not bound by the curves of those curled tresses
cannot become aware of the mystery of the lover's distress.

My heart takes pride in the approaching martyr who obeys destiny's order
and lays down his head before the sword without fear or sorrow.

Would that the poor Shaykh, so ignorant of religion and true learning,
could relinquish all his pride and forego his duplicity.

O 'Abdí, if only the eyes of the people had not become blind,
the one-eyed man would no longer wield the weapon of condemnation.[120]

Lo, had the glad tidings manifested by Bahá'u'lláh been in vain,
they would hardly have shone forth such world-conquering beams of light.

(14) BEYOND HEROIC LEGENDS: ON THE ANNIVERSARY OF THE MARTYRDOM OF THE BÁB[121]
BY 'ABDÍ

O crimson-breasted Bird,
O martyred Eagle[122] of love,
though Your blood was shed
by the oppression of the Shí'ih,

the clarion call of Your glad tidings
to the ears of every soul
is not gone from the hearts,
nor will it ever be!

O Thou Eminent[123] Spirit,
whose Temple had no resting place,
for fifty long years
after Your martyrdom;[124]

how wondrous that while in the palm
of the enemy's hand, You had no desire
but to offer up the pearl of Your life
for love of the Friend!

How astounding!
Those helpless foes
found need to martial troops
simply to slaughter You.

On that calamitous day of fatal shots,
the wind of destiny
scattered dust of the dark earth
upon the heads of onlookers.[125]

The bullet that aimed
at the heart of the Primal Point
struck pigeons perched
on the roof of the hram.[126]

Your chest, which was
the Qiblih of Mystery for Anís,
received row upon row of bullets
from oppression of the people of this age.

Finally, the fusillade, which
at the first try was itself ashamed
to approach the chest of that Temple,
that veritable throne of God,

at last tore it to pieces
on the second predestined round
so that the people of this age
might become humiliated in their shame.

But a century later these same people
have quite forgotten their dishonor,
have trampled upon that soil of your sacred court
for "spiritual" reward,

unaware that with the pickaxe
of their own ignorance they were
demolishing with their hands
the foundation of their own abode.[127]

By order of Sháh and Shaykh,
crowds were scattered and dispersed
anywhere they had gathered
because of the miracles You wrought.

It was the Shabdíz[128] of love
and the steed of intellectual pride,
the restive stallion,
that was tamed by Your presence.[129]

Yet the Shí'ih did not recognize You,
even though You came to them
accompanied with miracles,
with clear and apparent signs,

even though the degree of love and sacrifice
manifested by Anís and Hujjat,
by Quddús and Táhirih was a sufficient
miracle of God for the people of this age,

while those who dwell at the foot
of the minbar[130] and the mihráb[131]
conceal the truth and blame You
because they fear one another.

But Your heralds,
carefree and brave of heart,
are the flight feathers[132]
of fort Tabarsí.

Say: What have You done
to countermand the impious muftí
that causes him, like his father before him,
to become Your inveterate enemy?

What have You said
against religious laws
that warrants its courts
to imprison and slaughter?

Now, instead of Máh-Kú's darkness,
the night is illumined by the light
beaming from the dome and nave
of Your luminous shrine,

that blessed place where at dawn
the golden sun becomes
the chandelier of this shining sky
reflecting from Your rooftop.

I thought to compose a heroic epic
inscribed with the tears I have shed
so that on the earthly plane
it would become like a brilliant star,

but, alas, You are beyond epic poems.
You are in the earth
and on the scroll of the sky
and imprinted in human history.

(15) A Poem of Unity[133]
by Na'ím

O people, we are indeed all human beings.
We are all servants of the same just God.

And because we come from the same mother and father,
we are truly sisters and brothers to one another.

We all share the same form and countenance,
are fashioned from the same elements and divine essence,[134]

are shaped into the most perfect of forms,[135]
and are conceived in the most beauteous image.

If even the most ravenous of beasts will not
tear apart its own kindred, then why should we?

For ages people have endured the agony of hatred.
Let us now rejoice in our newfound amity and accord.

Dwelling as we do, one family in a small household,
how is it sensible to allow estrangement among us?

Unless we permit ourselves to be deceived by nefarious tyrants,
we must surely know that we are all the fruits of one tree.

Hearken to the resounding call of the Creator of the universe:
"Liberate the bound ones! Free the captive ones!"

(16) 'Abdu'l-Bahá in America[136] (1912)
by Na'ím

The country of Iran joyously sends to America
this heartfelt wish:

that the blessed arrival in your dominion
of the Center of the Covenant be blessed.

The eastern sun now rises in the West,
though the East is not darkened thereby

since the true Sign of the Unity of God –
who has no likeness, no partner, no peer –

has forged the East and the West into one land,
has made the Daylam and the Tájík one people.[137]

He has welded together the hearts so firmly
that throughout eternity they never will be parted.

For though East and West be divided by water and clay,
they are heart-to-heart and soul-to-soul.

He hath proclaimed it; therefore, so will it be
throughout every country and region, this command of the King:

that this is the promised time for the amity of humankind,
that the time for unity and accord has at long last arrived.

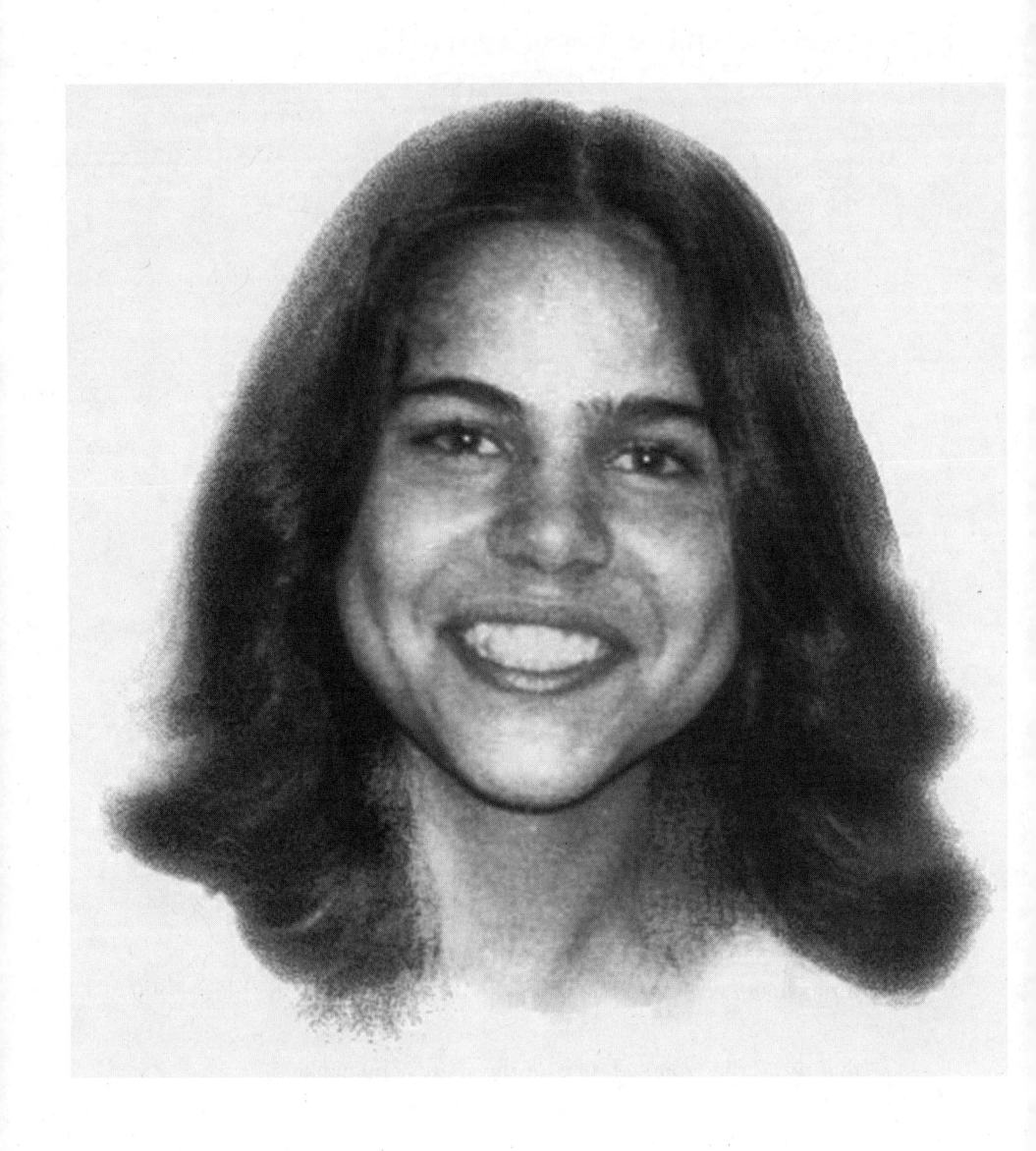

Muná Mahmúdnizhád

Part II: O You Who Claim to Believe

Background

Muná Mahmúdnizhád, seventeen years of age, was one of ten Bahá'í women executed in Shíráz on 18 June 1983. The charge against her was teaching Bahá'í classes to children in a private home. Her bright, smiling, beauteous countenance could surely charm the most hardened heart. But her look, so happy, so confident, belies her obstinate and unquenchable courage that so angered her interrogators. She scoffed at their threats, laughed at the suggestion that a mere word could save her from the waiting noose.

What could he do, the enraged mujtahid? How could he in his lofty station endure such a slight to his authority? And such love, such courage, such sacred beauty could prove incendiary were she returned to her family and the community of believers. She left him no choice.

In the end, she stood before the noose, smiled, and kissed the cord that would quickly draw her from this world to the realm of her beloved. And we, we who are left behind to gaze at those eyes, can only marvel at her victory and at our loss.

"The Bahá'í Question"[138] *An excerpt from* **The Bahá'í Question**

In searching for an historical analogy that adequately depicts the plight of the Bahá'ís of Iran, the New York Times compared the current policies of the Iranian government toward the Bahá'í community with the sinister Nuremberg Laws imposed by the Nazis in the 1930's, depriving German Jews of their rights.

Despite signs of political change in Iran, history shows that the Iranian government's systematic persecution of the Bahá'ís of Iran will not end without the full emancipation of the Bahá'ís, legal protection for their institutions, and explicit recognition of their right to exist as a religious community.

Throughout the last century and a half, the Bahá'ís of Iran have been persecuted for their religious beliefs. Despite the fact that they are committed to non-violence, tolerance and loyalty to government, they have been tortured, imprisoned, subjected to mob violence, and executed by fanatical elements of Iranian society, ranging from local clergy and their uneducated followers to, in this most recent 20-year period, government agents representing the highest levels of leadership.

With the triumph of the Islamic revolution in 1979, the persecution of Bahá'ís intensified as the government embarked on a systematic campaign to eradicate the Bahá'í community of Iran.

Between 1978 and 1998, more than 200 Bahá'ís were executed by the Iranian government. The majority of them were members of the community's democratically elected governing councils. During the 1980s especially, hundreds more Bahá'ís were imprisoned, and tens of thousands were deprived of jobs, pensions, businesses, and educational opportunities. Bahá'ís face these persecutions solely because of their religious beliefs.

In response to intense international pressure, the most notable example of which has been a series of United Nations resolutions against Iran, the Iranian government in the late 1980s reduced the rate of executions and the number of Bahá'ís held in prison.

Despite an apparent abatement of the most severe forms of persecution against the Bahá'ís in the 1990s, a close look at the evidence reveals that the government of the Islamic Republic of Iran still seeks to marginalize, suffocate and ultimately destroy the 350,000-member Bahá'í community, Iran's largest religious minority.

In July 1998, Mr. Rúhu'lláh Rawhání, a 52-year-old medical supplies salesman and father of four, was hanged in Mashhad. In July 1997, two other Bahá'ís, Mr. MásháIláh Enáyatí and Mr. Shahrám Rezá'í, were killed in unrelated incidents under circumstances related to their religious beliefs. And in March 1992, Mr. Bahman Samandarí, a well-known Bahá'í businessman in Tihrán, was summoned to Evín prison and summarily executed. As of early 1999, at least 16 Bahá'ís were being held in prison, with six facing death sentences.

Beyond the government's willingness to execute Bahá'ís and/or to allow them to be killed, clear evidence of the government's intentions emerged in early 1993 with the discovery of a hitherto secret Government memorandum aimed at establishing policy regarding "the Bahá'í question." Drafted by the Supreme Revolutionary Cultural Council and signed by President Ali Khamenei, the document lays out unequivocally the government's overall objective – to ensure that the "progress and development" of the Bahá'í community "shall be blocked."

The continuing force of that document, which calls for a series of restrictions on the access of Bahá'ís to education and livelihood that is nothing less than a blueprint for the strangulation of the Bahá'í community, was vividly demonstrated in September-October 1998 when government agents arrested some 36 Bahá'í

academics and raided more than 500 Bahá'í homes, confiscating hundreds of thousands of dollars worth of books, computers, and laboratory equipment. Witnesses describe some of the raiders as having been accompanied by film crews – evidence of the methodical nature of the attacks.

The aim of the assault was to shut down the Bahá'í Institute for Higher Education (BIHE), an effort by the Bahá'í community of Iran to provide university education for its young people, who have been systematically excluded from colleges and universities in Iran since the Islamic government came to power. Founded in 1987, the BIHE operated as an independent, full-fledged university with an enrollment of some 900 students, a faculty of more than 150 first-rate academics and instructors, and complete course offerings in ten subject areas such as engineering and accounting.

These raids and other actions contradict the government's oft-repeated contention that it has no campaign of persecution against the Bahá'ís. Given Iran's long history of measures taken against the Bahá'ís, the overall effect of the policies established by the memorandum and its continued fulfillment through sporadic executions, revolving door imprisonments, periodic arrests, and the general harassment aimed at Bahá'ís and their institutions provide clear evidence that Iran hopes to continue its oppression of the Bahá'í community of Iran while arousing as little foreign attention as possible.

As a result of this campaign, the Bahá'ís of Iran remain in a precarious state. They are denied the right to practice their faith freely, guaranteed under international human rights instruments such as the International Bill of Human Rights, to which Iran is a party. The administrative institutions of their Faith have been dismantled in accordance with a government edict. They live each day knowing that their government seeks to block their development as a community, and that even slight infractions can result in the deprivation of their livelihood, imprisonment or worse.

No one, however, has suggested that the Bahá'í community in Iran poses a threat to the Iranian authorities. The principles of the Bahá'í Faith require members to be obedient to their government and to avoid partisan political involvement, subversive activity, and all forms of violence. The community has sedulously avoided aligning itself in any fashion with any of the country's governments, ideologies or opposition movements.

Viewed objectively, the Iranian government's treatment of the Bahá'í community offers a singular litmus test as to whether the current political changes that are represented as reforms, altering the face of Iran, are genuine.

Bahá'ís Executed Since the Revolution

1978

1. Mr. Ahmad Ismá'ílí
2. Mr. Díyá'u'lláh Haqíqat
3. Mr. Shír-Muhammad Dastpísh
4. Mrs. 'Avad-Gul Fahandizh
5. Mr. Sifatu'lláh Fahandizh
6. Mr. Khusraw Afnání
7. Mr. Parvíz Afnání

1979

8. Mr. Ibráhím Ma'naví
9. Mr. Hájí-Muhmmad 'Azízí
10. Mr. Husayn Shakúrí
11. Mr. 'Alí-Akbar Khursandí
12. Mr. Bahár Vujdání
13. Mr. 'Alí Sattárzádíh
14. Mr. 'Azamatu'lláh Fahandizh

1980

15. Mr. Habíbu'lláh Panáhí
16. Mr. Ghulám-Husayn A'zamí
17. Mr. 'Alí-Akbar Mu'íní
18. Mr. Badi'u'lláh Yazdání
19. Mr. Parviz Bayání
20. Mr. Mir-Asadu'lláh Mukhtárí
21. Mr. Hasan Ismá'ílzádíh

22. Mr. Yúsuf Subhání
23. Mr. Yadu'lláh Ástání
24. Dr. Farámarz Samandarí
25. Mr. Muhammad Akbarí
26. Mr. Yadu'lláh Mahbubíyán
27. Mr. Dhabíhu'lláh Mu'miní
28. Mr. Núru'lláh Akhtar-Khávarí
29. Mr. 'Azízu'lláh Dhabíhíyán
30. Mr. Firaydún Farídání
31. Mr. Mahmúd Hasanzádíh
32. Mr. 'Abdu'l-Vahháb Kázimí-Manshádí
33. Mr. Jalál Mustaqím
34. Mr. 'Alá Mutahhari
35. Mr. Rídá Firúzí
36. Mr. Muhammad-Husayn Ma'súmí
37. Mrs. Shikkar-Nisá Ma'súmí
38. Mr. Bihrúz Saná'í

1981

39. Dr. Manúchihr Hakím
40. Mr. Mihdí Anvarí
41. Mr. Hidáyatu'lláh Dihqání
42. Mrs. Núráníyyih Yárshátir
43. Mr. Sattár Khushkhú
44. Mr. Ihsánu'lláh Mihdí-Zádih
45. Mr. Yadu'lláh Vahdat
46. Mr. Muhammad (Suhráb) Habíbí
47. Mr. Muhammad-Baqir (Suhayl) Habíbí
48. Mr. Husayn Khándil
49. Mr. Tarázu'lláh Khuzayn

50. Mr. Husayn Mutlaq
51. Dr. Fírúz Na'ímí
52. Dr. Nasir Vafá'í
53. Mr. Buzurg 'Alavíyán
54. Mr. Háshim Farnúsh
55. Mr. Farhang Mavaddat
56. Dr. Masíh Farhangí
57. Mr. Badí'u'lláh Faríd
58. Mr. Yadu'lláh Pústchí
59. Mr. Varqá Tibyáníyán (Tibyání)
60. Mr. Kamálu'd-Dín Bakhtávar
61. Mr. Ni'matu'llah Kátibpúr Shahídí
62. Mr. 'Abdu'l-'Alí Asadyárí
63. Mr. Husayn Asadu'lláh-Zadeh
64. Mr. Mihdí Báhirí
65. Dr. Masrúr Dakhílí
66. Dr. Parvíz Fírúzí
67. Mr. Manúchihr Khádi'í
68. Mr. Alláh-Virdí Mítháqí
69. Mr. Habíbu'lláh Tahqíqí
70. Mr. Ismá'íl Zihtáb
71. Mr. Husayn Rastigar-Námdár
72. Mr. Habíbu'llah 'Azízí
73. Mr. Bahman 'Atifí
74. Mr. 'Izzat 'Atifí
75. Mr. Ahmad Ridvání
76. Mr. Atá'u'lláh Rawhání
77. Mr. Gushtásb Thábit-Rásikh
78. Mr. Yadu'lláh Sipihr-Arfa

79. Mr. Mihdí Amín Amín
80. Mr. Jalál 'Azízí
81. Dr. 'Izzatu'lláh Furúhí
82. Mrs. Zhínús Ni'mat Mahmúdí
83. Dr. Mahmúd Majdhúb
84. Mr. Qudratu'lláh Rawhání
85. Dr. Sírús Rawshaní
86. Mr. Kámrán Samímí

1982

87. Mrs. Shíva Mahmúdí Asadu'llah-Zádih
88. Mr. Iskandar 'Azízí
89. Mrs. Shidrukh Amír-Kiyá Baqá
90. Mr. Fathu'lláh Firdawsí
91. Mr. Khusraw Muhandisí
92. Mr. Kúrush Talá'í
93. Mr. Atá'u'lláh Yávarí
94. Mr. Ibráhím Khayrkháh
95. Mr. Husayn Vahdat-i-Haq
96. Mr. 'Askar Muhammadí
97. Mr. Ihsánu'lláh Khayyámí
98. Mr. 'Azízu'lláh Gulshaní
99. Mrs. Ishráqiyyih Furúhar
100. Mr. Mahmúd Furúhar
101. Mr. Badí'u'lláh Haqpaykar
102. Mr. Ágáhu'lláh Tízfahm
103. Miss Jaláliyyih Mushta'il Uskú'í
104. Mrs. Irán Rahímpúr (Khurmá'í)
105. Mr. Nasru'lláh Amíní
106. Mr. Sa'du'lláh Bábázádih

107. Mr. 'Atá'u'lláh Haqqání
108. Mr. Muhammad Abbásí
109. Mr. Jadídu'lláh Ashraf
110. Manúchihr Farzánih Mu'ayyad
111. Mr. Muhammad Mansúrí
112. Mr. Manúchíhr Vafá'í
113. Mr. 'Abbás-'Ali Sádiqipúr
114. Mr. 'Alí Na'ímíyán
115. Mr. Habíbu'lláh Awjí
116. Mr. Dhíyá'u'lláh Ahrárí
117. Mr. Husayn Nayyírí-Isfahání
118. Mrs. Guldánih 'Alípúr

1983

119. Mr. Hidáyatu'lláh Síyávushí
120. Mr. Yadu'lláh Mahmúdnizhád
121. Mr. Rahmatu'lláh Vafá'í
122. Mrs. Túbá Zá'irpúr
123. Mr. 'Adadu'lláh (Azíz) Zaydí
124. Mr. Jalál Hakímán
125. Mr. Suhayl Safá'í
126. Dr. Bahrám Afnán
127. Mr. 'Abdu'l-Husayn Azádí
128. Mr. Kúrush Haqbín
129. Mr. 'Ináyatu'lláh Ishráqí
130. Mr. Jamshíd Síyávushí
131. Mr. Bahrám Yaldá'í
132. Miss Shahín (Shírín) Dálvand
133. Mrs. 'Izzat Jánamí Ishráqí
134. Miss Ru'yá Ishráqí

135. Miss Muná Mahmúdnizhád
136. Miss Zarrín Muqímí-Abyánih
137. Miss Mahshíd Nírúmand
138. Miss Símín Sábirí
139. Mrs. Táhirih Arjumandí Síyávushí
140. Miss Akhtar Thábit
141. Mrs. Nusrat Ghufrání Yaldá'í
142. Mr. Suhayl Húshmand
143. Mr. Ahmad-'Alí Thábít-Sarvístání
144. Mr. Muhammad Ishráqí
145. Mr. Akbar Haqíqí
146. Mr. Bahman Díhqání
147. Mr. 'Abdu'l-Majíd Mutahhar

1984

148. Mr. Rahmatu'lláh Hakímán
149. Mr. Ghulám-Husayn Hasanzádih-Shákirí
150. Mr. Muhsin Radaví
151. Mr. Nusratu'lláh Díyá'í
152. Mr. Kámrán Lutfí
153. Mr. Rahím Rahímíyán
154. Mr. Yadu'lláh Sábiríyán
155. Mr. Asadu'lláh Kámil-Muqaddam
156. Mr. Maqsúd 'Alízádih
157. Mr. Jalál Payraví
158. Mr. Jahángír Hidáyatí
159. Mr. 'Alí-Muhammad Zamání
160. Mr. Nusratu'lláh Vahdat
161. Mr. Ihsánu'lláh Kathírí
162. Dr. Manúchihr Rúhí

163. Mr. Amínu'lláh Qurbánpúr
164. Mr. Rustam Varjávandí
165. Mr. Shápúr (Húshang) Markazí
166. Mr. Fírúz Purdil
167. Mr. Ahmad Bashírí
168. Mr. Yúnis Nawrúzí-Iránzád
169. Mr. 'Alí Ridá Níyákán
170. Mr. Díyá'u'lláh Maní'í-Uskú'í
171. Dr. Farhád Asdaqí
172. Mr. Fírúz Atharí
173. Mr. Ghulám-Husayn Farhand
174. Mr. 'Ináyatu'lláh Haqíqí
175. Mr. Jamál Káshání
176. Mr. Jamshíd Púr-Ustádkár
177. Dr. Rúhu'lláh Ta'lím

1985

178. Mr. Rúhu'lláh Hasúrí
179. Mr. Rúhu'lláh Bahrámsháhí
180. Mr. Nusratu'lláh Subhání
181. Mr. 'Abbás Idilkhání
182. Mr. Rahmatu'lláh Vujdání
183. Mr. Núr'ud-Dín Tá'ifí
184. Mr. 'Azízu'lláh Ashjárí

1986

185. Mr. Paymán Subhání
186. Mr. Sirru'lláh Vahdat-Nizámí
187. Mr. Fidrus Shabrukh
188. Mr. Faríd Bihmardí
189. Mr. Habíbu'lláh Muhtadí

190. Mr. Bábak Tálibí
191. Mr. Iraj Mihdí-Nizhád
 1987

192. Mr. Ahmad Kávih
193. Mr. Surúsh Jabbárí
194. Mr. 'Abu'l-Qásim Sháyiq
195. Mr. Ardishír Akhtarí
196. Mr. Amír-Husayn Nádirí
 1988

197. Mr. Bihnám Páshá'í
198. Mr. Iraj Afshín
199. Mr. Mihrdad Maqsudí
 1992

200. Mr. Bahman Samandarí
201. Mr. Rúhu'lláh Ghidamí
 1995

202. Mr. Shirvín Falláh
 1997

203. Mr. Mansúr Dawlat
204. Mr. Shahrám Rizá'í
205. Mr. Máshá'lláh 'Ináyatí
 1998

206. Mr. Rúhu'lláh Rawhání

(17) Do Not Lay Waste Our Home Again![139]
by 'Abdí

O Muslim, do not make us homeless and destitute.
May your house prosper, but do not lay waste our home again.

O Magistrate of the true Faith, do not make the eyes of Bahá'í children
so red with tears in separation from their own mothers.

May you relish your triumph and victory, but do not make
homeless ones wander once more as contemptible vagrants.

O Muslims, if you oppress the peoples of the world,
do not then call yourselves descendants of 'Alí, the Sháh-i-Javánmardán.[140]

Murder and plunder are not the law of the faith of Mustafá![141]
If you believe not in religion, do not justify yourselves with the Qur'án.

O Shaykh, for a moment consider your decree and entrust not your religion
to the judgment of the base and ignorant ones in your midst.

Do not fan the fire of enmity and oppression more grievously!
Do not render the hearts of God's creatures devoid of conscience!

With a bloody heart and a fiery sigh, 'Abdí said,
"O Muslim, do not lay waste our home again."

(18) O Ye That Are Foolish, Yet Have a Name to be Wise[142]
by 'Abdí

Though the prelates and clerics may close the tavern doors,
they have opened the rear door to the alleyway of hypocrisy and deceit.

O alas that this oppressive sect has, like past generations,
torn asunder the mantle of modesty and respect.

Alas, behold how this iniquitous tribe has slaughtered
the most innocent servants of God.

The cries and sighs of the martyrs of Bahá
echo from my breast, which desires only the arrow of calamity.

O Shaykh, strike as repeatedly as you wish with your taunts,
with arrows of oppression the caravan of the people of Bahá.

But be wary of heedlessness! For if there is a God,
He will harken to the moaning of our hearts at prayer time.

If there be no commentary about loyalty in your lexicon of questions,[143]
surely there must be a limit[144] set for injustice and oppression.

O 'Abdí, were the tyrannous Shaykh to recognize God,
he would cease this tribulation and become truly learned.

(19) Seize the Sure Handle[144]
by Dr. Valíyu'llá Kamál Ábádí

We have no dealings with the world
or with those who desire it;
nothing occupies our thoughts
save the love of the countenance of Abhá!

In our hearts there exists neither love of worldly things
nor hatred nor animus for any existent entity;
in our hearts there is no room for aught else
save love of the Beloved.

We fear not any calamity –
indeed, our lives hunger for this pain;[145]
we seek no remedy or cure
for the pain of the love of the Beloved.

Do not threaten us with
the wave's tumult or storm's surge;
the water has already surged above our heads.
We have no fear of the sea!

You falsely accuse us of being strangers here!
You call us "spies" for a foreign land!
Verily, we are eager to inform whoever will hear
that our love embraces the whole world!

We are friends, brothers, helpmates
to all the peoples and nations!
We have no quarrel or contention
with anyone in the world.

When has defiance or dissent
ever been found to befit us.
Ever do we avoid rancor and strife;
We are loving friends to all the peoples.

Lo, the infallible Qur'án itself says:
"Let there be no compulsion in religion"[146]
O ye magnanimous ones, we can devise
no better counsel than this.

We desire no refuge, no shelter
other than the recognition of Truth,[147]
while you, alas, are to be pitied, shackled as you are
by your own caprice and vain imaginings.

O Haqqáni, become shackled instead to the
one true faith, the religion of God,
for there is nothing better and more secure
for anyone than this "Sure Handle"![148]

(20) Questions of the Heart[149]
by 'Abdí

When the phoenix of love
entered my heart,
the sparrow of wisdom
fled to the realm of non-existence.

As the Hidden Treasure[150]
viewed Himself in the mirror,
He opened His veil
and conjoined spirit with form.[151]

What did that pure essence
of love's sacrifice see
that He wrote this story
in the book of existence?

Who is he who with his own soul's
burning martyrdom,
set ablaze the soul of his mother
and the holy family?[152]

Who, like a bloody tulip
at the feet of the Cypress
with sorrowing heart laid his head
at the feet of the Blessed Beauty?

That was the Purest Branch who,
before his martyrdom,
placed his life on the path of the Beloved
with pen and tablet.

Did you see how the fire
that burned the body of Badí'
eternally branded the face
of the king of Persia?

When Satan was defeated
in the war against truth,
he picked up the Qur'án
and stamped his oath upon it.

O 'Abdí, in His eternal wisdom
the Ancient Cupbearer also poured
a sip from the sweet wine of sorrows
into the goblet of your rejoicing.

(21) The Tavern of Love[153]
by 'Abdí

If the breeze of the flower garden of 'Ábádih[154] attracts your heart,
it is from the fragrance scented by the dew of the red blossoms of Nayríz.

If in that Garden of the Merciful,[155] the leaf of the anemone seems
to shoot out sparks, it is the flame of the red blood of the faithful ones.

O Cupbearer, there is no path from the tavern except that of martyrdom
now that your drunken eyes have brought about such shedding of blood!

Since my goblet of patience overflows with these tears,
pour the red wine of faná[156] into the goblet of love.

Did Sabá the wind make a pilgrimage to your quarter
so that, like the musk of Khutan, your scent is attracting the hearts?

You are our spring, O Flower, since without You on the horizon,
the morning dawn of springtime would be like the sunset of autumn.

O King, bestow a look at this beggar with the eyes of Your benevolence,
since he is deserving of an affectionate glance.

If 'Abdí still passes his life in Your quarter,
it is only because his life is unworthy of sacrifice for Your sake.

(22) Becoming a Wayfarer: Yesterday, Today, and Tomorrow[157]
ANONYMOUS

If you ask me who I am today
I am both tomorrow and the "Alast."[158]

Tomorrow I will not be what I am today,
and I am not now what I was last night.

Since I am drunk with the wine of wayfaring today,
how can I tie my feet to a place of rest or leisure?[159]

Though I be minuscule and petty today,
my goal is to aspire forever towards perfection.

Since I have rent asunder all the bonds from my soul today,
tell me not that all things are predetermined.[160]

I flew from the roof of this age today –
a bird soaring in the realm of the garden of mystery.[161]

Since I escaped from the limitation of all hesitancy today,
why should I seek out contentment or rest?

I shall not cease treading this path today,
for our life's story is ever wayfaring and becoming.[162]

Alas, the weight of my words broke my pen today,
but so many are the mysteries still unrevealed in my heart.

(23) Prison Alchemy [163]
by Muhammad Ridá Hisámí (Imprisoned seven years)

How delightful is the resplendent prison courtyard!
How pleasant the air in this prison world!

How grateful am I at dawn in this secluded corner,
intoning the prayers and sacred words of God,

meditating on the Friend after receiving the jailer's decree,
becoming intoxicated by the wine of this place,

calling to mind the army[164] of martyrs,
those flower petals fluttering to the floor of this jail.

Where did it go – the melodious-voiced bird of this jail?
From the storm of calamity to gardens and groves!

So many a Majnún in these solitary rooms
lay burning in the fire of Laylí's gloom.

"When would hearing a tale be equal to seeing it?"[165]
Can imagining imprisonment ever be the same as being here?

By His Holiness the Báb, the Prisoner of Chihríq,
the exalted, the supreme 'Alí[166] of imprisonment,

By that Ancient Essence of the "Most Great Prison,"[167]
the Blessed Beauty, the Abhá of imprisonment,

By the Most Great Branch, that Master of the world,
who has dwelt a lifetime in the prison of 'Akká,

By that "Chosen Branch,"[168] the astute and powerful one,
the executor and most cherished[169] Guardian[170] of the Akká prison,

By each of these, prison becomes a flower-garden to Hisámí, so long as the Lord of this prison is pleased with me.[171]

(24) True Courage[172]
by Fakhru'd-Din Húshang Rawhání (Sarkish)

To become detached from one's own life
requires courage, resolve:
to bear the pangs of prison life,
to remain steadfast in the Covenant,

to become afire from head to toe,
to give your life for love of the Beloved,
suddenly to cast aside entirely
every affection for this world,

to become intimate with despair,
to become felicitous in calamities,
to close the heart's eye to whatever
is not from the Friend.

(25) Those Who Keep the Vigil[173]
by Bihrúz Bihishtí

Those who cast their lives in the path of the Beloved
are free from the prison of time and space,

are drowned in light from the rays of Bahá.
Like the face of the sun in the sky, they radiate beams of light.

On the path of calamity they lead the caravan of contentment.
In love and loyalty, they are the signs of this time, of this age.

In the marketplace of sacrifice, they beat the drum of martyrdom.
They have no wish except to seek out the Friend.

In the heights of truth they open the wings of mystery, hovering, tranquil,
reposed, detached from superstition and vain imaginings.

They fear not the downpour from the storm of oppression,
for they are the vast sea that roars from shore to shore.

In the dark night of the winter solstice of calamity,
they are not frightened by the hateful bat, but are vigilant.

Although they may be captured and enslaved in the earthly realm,
they are kings adorned with regal crowns in the realm of the soul.

In the earthly planes of faná they are slain and fallen.
In the kingdom of baqá they remain ever alive and eternal.

(26) THE CODE OF AN EXILE IN THE CAUSE OF GOD[174]
BY SÁLIHZÁDIH SAMARQANDÍ (DIED IN EXILE TO SIBERIA)

Because I am deserving,
I cannot become destitute;
I will never be terrified
by the rumors of others,

by those cowards who utter
sophistry and nonsense:
I am like the courageous lion
and will never become fearful.

I am no child –
I need no schooling –
for I have absorbed the Iqán
and the lessons of love.

I am a true Bahá'í,
a servant of the one Truth
and thus will not become like you,
a sycophant seeking favors.

Since my utterance is
but the word of God,
I will have no need
to seize you by the collar.[175]

I am truth-telling, truth-accepting,
truth-searching and truth-natured.
Therefore, in truth, I will never
become a source of deceit.

So long as the sorrowing soul
has chosen my body for its abode,
I will never be the cause of sadness
to any other heart.

Because of my promise, my covenant,
I will be steadfast as a mountain;
Neither will I tremble at the
lightning or the winds of turmoil.

Since my utterance is completely true
for people of the heart,
I will not become a target
for the arrows of sarcasm and calumny.

If a hundred thousand calamities
appear on the horizon,
my mind is so resolute
that I will not become distracted.

Even should the world itself
sink into a stormy maelstrom,
I will be like Noah and never drown
in the fathomless ocean of storms.

(27) STANDING IN THE NEED OF PRAYER[176]
by 'Abdí

So long as we are servants
with heart and soul at the threshold of Bahá,
we shall be free from the bonds
of the cage of desire and caprice.

In the flower garden of the world of existence
we are intoxicated like spring birds,
more light-winged than
Sabá the east wind.

In any place where the candle
of love is luminous,
we are those heart-singed moths
at the banquet of fidelity.

Whenever the cruel enemy
commits diabolic injustice and torture,
we stand with hearts in hand
eager and ready in the field of sacrifice.

We are dwellers in the tavern of love,[177]
and so it is that we remain
remote from the back alleys
of duplicity and imposture.

Though in the midst of the
storm-tossed sea of divine calamities,
we find restful ease because
we are content with the will of God.

O 'Abdí, do you think
that it is because of the bounty of prayer
that we inhabit the Supreme Empyrean
and are beloved of God?

Far be it for God to have need
of our prayer and praise!
It is we who stand in need
of prayer and supplication.

(28) The Cup of Calamity
by Fakhru'd-Dín Húshang Rowhání (Sarkish)

"I thirst for the cup of calamity;
I have no fear of Satan –
those weak in the Covenant
fear for their lives, not I.

"O Tranquility of my soul,
whether You push me away
or call me into Your presence,
I have no refuge but the hem of Your robe.[178]

"So long as I have Your love in my heart,
I need not have fear of anyone!
So long as You are my Faithful Friend,
no enemy can discomfit me.

"How felicitous is treading this path of union,
offering up my sweet life.
But though I possess the feet to walk,
I have not yet the will to persevere.

"I can scarcely bear any more
grievous atrocities and gross injustice
of these seditious ones,
but I will deny them my wailing and weeping.

"The blade is now in enemy hands.
The jealous ones have issued the decree.
Yet under the threat of their blade,
I find I fear not for body or soul.

"You need try no more to frighten
away my soul, weltered in pain:
my heart fears no oppressors now,
no more than the prick of pin.

"O he who became astonished
at my endurance and fortitude,
behold on my body no coat of mail,
only the garment of faith.

"Moment by moment waves of divine
assistance reach me, assuage me,
else I would not have this perseverance
against such a ruinous flood.

"O ye prosperous ones of the earth,
may the coin of existence be freely yours!
As for me, no part of this garden have I
save the thorn of injustice."

His soul thus afire in the ocean of calamity,
Sarkash uttered then these words:
"I thirst for the cup of calamity!
I have no fear of Satan!"

(29) Awjí's Istiqbál of the Mazih Dárad[179]
by Awjí (martyred)

O my soul, losing my life
in Your path would be delightful!
Losing one's life in the path
of the Beloved is delightful!

Becoming debased and infamous
for being accused of loving You,
sinless and innocent while sitting in the
corner of a cell, would be delightful!

In the corner of the cell
with dear ones during visitation,
picking flowers, speaking flowers
and laughing, is delightful![180]

Receiving salty smiles[181]
from the lips of the friends,
and sugar from the mines of
salt would be delightful!

Kicking, cursing, blows to my face
are hardly charming:
lashes of tribulation on my
naked body are delightful!

This assemblage is disheveled
in remembrance of Your tresses,
yet the consternation[182] of this
bewildered entourage is delightful!

O Nábit, flee from the side of
those whose souls are lethargic;[183]
the body lying lifeless on the ground
without its soul would be delightful!

(30) Don the Crimson Robe[184]
by Husayn Qaráchidághí

If you are intoxicated with the Beloved,
cast off the robe of existence from your body
since such a lowly garment
is hardly fit for a lover.

If you are one of the truly learned,[185]
remove the robe of your vain imaginings
and don instead a robe of red
created from martyrs' blood.

Since this robe is made of purity
fashioned precisely for your body,
come place it upon your shoulders,
this robe of truth.

Behold now this refined garment[186] of unity
which has become so elegant on your body!
Since you have won this honor with your labor,
take care that you not lose it carelessly.

Nowhere in the universe will you find silk like this,
nor is there gold embroidery like it.
Its warp is gnostic knowledge;
its woof is divine certitude.

Only from the hands of a wise elder
could such fabric be fashioned,
because the cunning Tailor
has no peer in all this world.

This robe is from a Kingdom
whose King is Ábhá.
It will never need mending,
nor can it ever be worn out.

It will exhibit such freshness
in the manifest and in the hidden realms
because every moment its splendor increases,
nor can its magnificence ever fade.

Because it will never become soiled,
it will ever be pleasant to behold.
O blessed be such an eternal gown
that can envelop the ethereal body.

(31) Song of the Immortal Phoenix[187]
by Dr. Sírús Rowshaní (martyred)

So long as I can lay my head at Your feet, O Friend,
how easily I would give up my life in the path of Your Faith –

a long life spent in this constant longing to see You.
Give me another life, and I will spend it just the same.

There is naught in the mirror of my heart but the Beloved's face.
I have nothing else to treasure except this Priceless Pearl.[188]

Whether You nourish me out of grace or seize from justice,
I am bound by Your bonds and caught in Your trap.

So long as service to Your Faith is my virtue and my perfection,
what need have I for worldly ornaments and wealth?

Your moonlike face is but the mirror of the Daystar.
Your raven hair brings to mind my darkest night.

Each person searches for his heart's desire, the object of his longing.
The "pious" ones seek after gold; I seek after the Friend.

An "immortal phoenix" informed of "the mount of faithfulness"[189]
and that lovely glad tiding bereft my heart of patience.

I am but a dark cloud, but I am from the springtime of the Beloved.
I am rain and I descend on flowers and thorns alike,

for there can be no rose in the garden without a thorn.
O unblossomed bud, caress me – who am but a thorn.

The honey of my words is so delightful to the palate
so long as I encounter a sweet night with You.

From that wine of the Vintner of Truth contained in the cask of Love,
give me a cup, O Eternal Wine-Giver, since I am half-drunk.

What station this is, to be the envy of mulk and malakút![190]
Truly, I am Cyrus, and yet but a speck of dust at the threshold of love.[191]

(32) WAITING FOR ASCENT[192]
ANONYMOUS

Happy shall be the day I withdraw
my hands from both wet and dry
and my head will rise like flames
in the blessed air of the Friend.[193]

I shall leave behind the dark world
for all the dark-hearted ones;
I shall pack my clothing and ascend
into the world of the dawn.

I shall burst asunder the four
worn walls of my frail body[194]
and fly from this feeble cage
to the immortal flower garden.

To the bird that is truly free,
meagre seeds of this world are unsatisfying.
Indeed, I shall hike up my skirt
from the perilous trap of earthliness.[195]

In the sanctuary of God's holiness
I shall wave about my hands in joy!
I shall drink the choice wine
from the goblet full of sparks!

I shall move aside the curtain
from the face of the Beloved!
I will become roaring drunk
from the joy of this visitation!

Like a compass tracing circles
around the point of the Beloved's beauty spot,
I will draw a boundary to blot out all else,
whether of heaven or of earth.

(33) THE FIERY HEART[196]
BY 'ABDÍ

After uttering
his praises to
the Beloved
of the world,
the martyr of love
spoke to the
head of the
firing squad:

"O valiant soldier,
think not
that from
your rage
this bullet hastens
to me with
your message
of hatred;

"The speed
derives from
this breast of mine
which rushes
fearlessly towards
your bullet
with a fiery
heart."

(34) A Martyr's Name[197]
by Fakhru'd-Dín Húshang Rawhání (Sarkish)

Calamity's tornado churned
malice in every alley, making
the dust of injustice settle
over doors and walls of homes;
the odor of ignorance and prejudice
arose from the earth, leaving its
scent in every quarter.

Yet again another innocent dove
rolled in his own blood.
Yet again there arose the wolves
howling for joy at seeing
the color of such carnage.
For Satan the day turned into
a time for delight and rejoicing.

Again the darkness of oppression
overshadowed the path of light
and the dissolute hand of injustice
plucked from earth's bosom
a newly blossomed flower,
snapping its fresh stem.

So pure was that blessed dove
that it soared all the way to paradise!
So blessed was paradise
that yet again a martyr's name
was written on its door.

(35) So Let it Be![198]
by Manúchihr Hijází

The soul in its dance flew to paradise.
So be it!
The vacant corpse was dragged across the bazaar.
So be it.

Why try to discover a hint of logic
in the spiritual path of the lover?
One who has lost his heart leaves no trace or name!
So be it.

So long as the storms of calamity unearth not
the roots of your zeal,
let the rough winds pluck leaves from your branches!
So be it!

So long as the soul becomes neither tarnished nor shamed –
which would be such a pity –
what matters if the body becomes bait for knives and scorn!
So be it!

So long as waters rush not beneath
those sturdy foundations of your culture,
what matter if the floods invade your cottage?
So be it!

So long as none can seize from you
the freedom of your belief,
what matters if chains of captivity come?
So be it!

I bequeath to you naught
save this well-wrought verse,
together with my life which has been offered up!
So be it!

(36) Epitaph[199]
by Fakhru'd-Dín Húshang Rawhání (Sarkish)
in memory of the martyr 'Atá'u'lláh Yávarí

O eternal beauty who hath flown off,
who hath ascended to the Throne of Grandeur,

O eternal beauty who swept up to the summits
beside the Dwelling Place of Loyalty,

O thou who hast attained the rank of those
who occupy the seats of honor in the High Hall,

O thou companion of all the beauteous souls,
the self-sacrificing ones,[200]

O thou conqueror of the highest heights of love,
O thou who hast achieved the summit itself,

O thou eternal beauty, whose magnanimity and servitude
were being fashioned in your kind heart,

O thou better than good, we cannot believe,
we cannot believe you have severed yourself from us.

O eternal beauty who hast vanished and absconded with
all the strength and patience that was in our hearts,

our eyes will be ever fixed on those distant paths;
until the last moments of our lives we will shoulder the burden of sorrow.

Though you and your beloved spouse are parted,
your souls are one, even as your hearts were one.

In her ear she ever hears your warm melodies,
sustained only by recalling memories of you.

Until now she had only read stories of grievous loves,
but she herself could not endure to be branded with such pain.

Until now she had heard only stories of such separated lovers,
but she had never witnessed such severance with her own eyes.

So she listens to your son Payám[201] speaking
and hears those same melodies that refreshed your heart,

she, with her broken heart and tear-filled eyes.
So many are the plaints she utters with silent lips.

Now it is your gentle child who is the hope of our hearts,
rekindling and vivifying cherished memories of you,

becoming a fine wine to be poured into our goblets,
tasting of delightsome honey to the palate,

becoming a light to illumine these dark nights
as he speaks of Love everlasting and eternal.

His presence brings us vivid recollections of you.
And since Payám brings to mind your love,

he, too, is another 'Atá[202] from God's mercy,
reminding us of your face, your hair, your traits.

Whatever possesses your fragrance is good.
So your young child shall for many years to come

embody your memory in our hearts and minds.
Like you, he talks of a love, eternal and everlasting.

'Atá'u'lláh Yávarí, never fear that you will be forgotten:
both your memory and your name live on.

(37) Entering the Holy City[203]
by Shápúr Markazí[204] (martyred)

I know not why my heart
is so vexed,
drumming so hard and fast.

Ah, my being has been ensnared again
by deep and boundless sadness
for which there seems to be no end.

Yet again the sword of my sinfulness
has delivered a mortal blow,
severing the cord of my faith.[205]

So despairing, so deranged am I
that my soul has become bereft
of any source of light.

Yesterday, my eyes were ever awash
in weary tears,
always watching the prison door.

In my mind's eye images of dear ones
appeared there, bright and shining,
the faces of son and daughter.

At last the power of my hope
produced bountiful fruit;
my guard said that I had visitors!

I embraced firmly those so dear
to my heart and soul until the guard
pronounced the ultimate pain:

This was farewell!
My burning heart became inflamed with sorrow,
the herald of a thousand further sorrows.

Light left my eyes as my soul
departed from my breast:
"these precious two are my life, my existence!

"There is no further need of
waiting at the door. Have I nothing left
but privation and despair?"

Trust, O Heart, in the benevolence of the Beloved!
Pray that your life will soon
depart this shell,

that you may become a sacrifice
for His Holiness, the Beloved, and no longer abide
with these bleak companions, Pain and Despair!

Entrust your dear ones to God
then follow the brave path,
O you who claim to believe!

Relinquish now all thoughts of those dear ones
so that you may dispense
with all earthly sorrow and pain!

(38) Acquiescence to God's Will[206]
by Nábit (martyred)

O joyous be that moment when bullets course towards my heart!
What grief I shall endure should my destiny's decree be forestalled!

The very blood of God's suffering lovers wields such mighty power
that through its force the Kingdom of Love can conquer the world.

While on this perilous path, the heart is constantly struggling
to seize the garment of the soul and never loosen its grasp.

Through this love, old ones become young again,
while remoteness from the Beloved ages each bright youth.

The thirsting ones search for flowing water, while the lover
is sated with this life by the fiery fever of attraction.

I have had a dream, and I trust that soon the Friend
becomes kind to me and makes the dream come true.[207]

So it is that the mujtahid has condemned me to sweet death.
O God, let there be no delay in this!

It would be apt for these base ones to deem me an infidel
were I, Nábit, to cry out like Mansúr, "I am God!"[208]

(39) A Daughter's Dream[209]
In memory of Shídrukh
by 'Abdí

"Forgive me, mother, that on this anniversary of your martyrdom
I have not scattered flower petals of my tears for you.

Forgive me, mother, that from these soul-searing tears,
not one drop have I scattered upon your grave.

Tell me, mother, how did your faithful heart become
a target for these people of oppression even when,

in the steadfastness of affection, your pure soul held in its palm
the pearl of life itself as barter for love?

O shooters of that fiery shower, that fusillade, forbear!
Know you not the grievous tyranny you commit?

Now that you have slaughtered in accordance with impious decrees,
why then need you desecrate the graves of those same corpses?

O Qiblih of the world of creation, look! See what people
are doing because of their hatred and detestation!

While we offer loyalty and beckon them with service and love,
see how the creatures of this age respond to us!

O soul-searing bullets, since this is my own dear mother,
can you not forbear seeking out the blood of this dear one?

This delicate dove – so innocent, so chaste and sinless –
is not only my mother, but also the crown that adorns my head!"[210]

Thus the martyr's daughter spoke and thus she shed her tears
that dropped like pearls into the lap of the moonlight.

And after the moon and Venus went into a deep sleep,
and the daughter's weary and sorrowing eyes were shut,

the favored child ascended from the world of clay
higher than the heavens and into the world of dreams.

With love she witnessed there her mother's beauteous countenance
clearer than in a mirror and encircled in a halo of light.

The smiling lips of that angelic face then opened
like a blossom kissed by a breeze in spring:

"O dear daughter of mine, O beloved light of my eyes,
O thou whose tear drops are like the fountains of paradise,

"you thought the tyrannical arrows of the wretched ones
freed my soul from the prison that is the earthly realm,

"but you were unaware that for the sake of reunion with the Friend,
my thirsty soul longed for that place of martyrdom, of sacrifice.

"My soul, sad and weary in the murderous prison cell,
was fevered by torment and a slave to torture.

"My face was blackened with bruises from blows of hands,
and my back ached from the brand and lashing of the whip

"until my weary and sorrowing soul could seek rest
only in the holy tabernacles of the heavenly abode

"when the pen of destiny inscribed my name in the red tablet
and my suffering and waiting at long last ceased.

"Now observe how angels stand rank upon rank to praise me,
all the way up to the throne of the King of the Eternal Abode,

and along with the song of angels sing a host of heavenly birds
warbling hymns of welcome and praise and glad-tidings of reunion."

Then from a lofty chamber[211] fashioned from the silken light
the desired and predestined Sháhid[212] was made manifest saying:

"O Heavenly and distinguished martyr,
reveal this to all the people of the earth in this age!

"Say: 'Auspicious be the destiny of women since, by means of
their loving souls, they have surpassed men, have won the victory.

"'See now how the phoenix of good fortune has spread open so wonderfully
the wings of women, that had been fettered, in the heaven of this Faith.'"

"Daughter, true you are now from the proud lineage of martyrs,
but know that the heritage I bequeathed you is even greater,

"for in the lofty place where dwell the angels on high
a choral cry calls out from thirty thousand martyrs:

"'Though the station of martyrdom bequeathed by the
　　　　Friend's benevolence
is a glorious robe of honor, a crown of great felicity,

"'the act of arising to serve His Cause with selflessness and sincerity
is a rank higher and more lofty than the station of martyrdom itself!'"

(40) MUNÁ[213]
BY 'ABDÍ

If my holy Beloved should
rise from His place again,
a roar of love would issue forth from
the earth where martyrs lie.

If a breeze should blow from the
disheveled tresses of the Beautiful One,
the fragrance of flowers would again
be carried by the wind of Sabá.

If the lover with flowing tears
were unable to rise to her feet,
she would grasp the robe
of the mighty Cypress.

If the envious one with his chains
could subdue the Sun of the universe,
the holy call would still be raised
from the corner of the Black Pit.[214]

Even were a hundred arrows
of calamity to be unloosed,
the lover's head would become
a shield for the Beloved's breast.[215]

It is a bounty to the family of Mahmúdnizhád
that from among tulip faces,
from amongst the true lovers,
one like Muná has arisen.

The moth while still burning
was saying: "In the fire of love
the anguished cry of yearning
will rise from our ashes!"

O 'Abdí, complain not about the enemy,
for the cries of deliverance
are heard emerging from the voices
of the blood of the martyrs of Bahá.

(41) THE MARTYR'S MESSAGE[216]
BY 'AZÍZ HAKÍMÍYAN

In the silence of moments,
in the heart of thoughts,
from the sound of Farháds' axes,[217]
in the region of remembrances,
from the songs of the wind,
on top of the gallows tree,[218]
in the flower and in the meadow
and in the garden and tulip field,
from the hearts of lovers
made impatient by their sorrows,
in the midst of blood and earth,
in the midst of tears of the vine,
from the darkness of the night
and from the bright of the morn,
there is, O martyr,
the mystery of your message.

(42) In Remembrance: The Free One[219]
by 'Abdí

The lover who has had no longing for life
has had no wish, save reunion with the Friend.

The enamored martyr, scattering his blood so easily,
has had no fear of the hatred or anger of the enemies.

The rain, invoking thunder amid the storm of misfortune,
has had no trepidation of the waves and terror of the sea.

The immortal bird, soaring amid the vastness of the heavens,
has had no destination save the eternal nest of the Phoenix.

Happy the thirsting heart on the day of its martyrdom
that has had in its glazed cup naught save the wine of love.

Never has so much attention been evoked in East or West
as the night cry of martyrs shouting, "O Bahá!"

The deft eagle downed by a fiery shower of rifle shot
has never had such an honorable and beauteous death!

In the season of spring, the path beside the edge of plains
has never had such red tulips in the time of flowering.

The garden of Iram[220] in the Loftiest Paradise
has not had such flower buds as have blossomed this day in Iran.

Though this world be a house of sorrow, the home of the crow,
behold how the Eagle of Love has never cared for this realm.

Truly, the Bahá'í has never laid claim to this realm of clay,
for truly free is one who has never become enamored of the world.

(43) THE DATE PALM LAMENTS ITS FRUIT[221]
BY 'ABDÍ

When we are remote from Your face,
there is no dawn for our night;
but for Your countenance,
there would be no light for our morning.

For me there is no companionship
with the moth of love;
I am a silent candle
whose sigh raises no flame.

Would that I could become
a handful of dust in the wind's hand;
only in this way would there be
a chance for me to pass by Your quarter.

I am a captive bird sorrowing
in separation from the Friend,
but though I possess neither wings nor feathers,
I have a song issuing forth from my heart.

Alas, in my exile from the
homeland of the Beloved,
except for reports of deaths of dear ones,
there is no news at all.

Alas! The corpses of these
Bahá'í martyrs have become
so trampled upon that now
there remains no sign of them.

The date palm is pelted by stones
because of the fruit it bears;
but bearing no fruit,
the thorn remains tranquil.

O 'Abdí, a heart filled with arrogance
but empty of love
is an oyster in a shell
containing no pearl within.

(44) BIRDS[222]
BY 'ABDÍ

1.

We are that very same captive bird they slaughter
on the night of mourning or at the day of the wedding feast.

2.

We harbor no fear of the maelstrom of wave's tumult:
when would a bird with a sea-heart[223] have any dread of a storm?

3.

'Ayyúb himself[224] did not have the patience and endurance
for such trouble and torment as they inflict upon us.

4.

So many humiliations which one day transmuted into eternal wealth:
we have observed the world-beaming morning during a night of sorrow.

(45) What Do They Want from Us?[225]
by 'Abdí

I know not what more these people desire from us!
What else do they desire from these captives of calamity?
What do they want?

From this handful of weak, distressed and wandering ones
who have sacrificed their existence to the winds of destruction,
what else do they want?

For a hundred and thirty years they have slaughtered and burned
the bodies of martyrs. What more do they now
want from the people of Bahá?

For the sake of God, should not one oppressor
at least ask another oppressor what else they want
from these perplexed souls?

From that delicate, orphaned, broken-hearted child
snatched from its mother's lap,
what do they want?

From that old, disabled, and grieving one
whose slaughtered son has turned a cottage into a house of mourning,
what more could they want?

If in their animosity they have condemned and confiscated a man
from his child or from the lonely spouse of that poor one,
what do they want from us?

Why does not some fair-minded soul finally ask these oppressors
what more they could want? "What do you want"?
What more could they possibly want?

(46) MEDITATION BEFORE DEATH[226]
BY FARAHMAND MUQBILÍN (ILHÁM)

O saddened heart,
become happy again;
leave those ruins;
become prosperous.

O saddened soul,
weary little sparrow,
fly from the corner of your cage.
Become free!

How long will you pound
the seal of silence on your lips?[227]
Break this quietude!
Become a cry!

The dark night of sorrow
is over now!
O blackened visage, O injustice,
vanish with the wind!

Another message
has arrived from the Friend:
"O Paradise of longing,
become established!

Wash away any trace of rust
or sadness from the soul!
Become the felicity
of every grieving thrall!

That martyr's blood
with its rosy hue was not wasted!
Become opulent, a mighty wave!
Become magnificent!"

O thou Mighty Cause,
as you take shape in the mind,
blot out from our memories
all vestiges of doubt.

O Ilhám, there is for you
no greater opportunity than this –
to become a source of elation
for all the ancestors who await you!

(47) The Terraces of Carmel: In Remembrance of the Báb[228]
ANONYMOUS

What is this paradise on God's Holy Mountain,
ascending step by step to the Throne of Grandeur,

this garden hanging in the sky,
the refined stones blended in variegated colors,

the green sward embracing its flowers,
the bubbling springs and fountains?

The hillside is blanketed, emblazoned with pansies,
the bushes ornamented with crowns of blossoms.

Coquettish cypresses have queued up
to be shaped in waves by morning breeze.

When the wind passes through the garden heights,
it ferries familiar perfume from the sour oranges of Shíráz[229]

calling to mind the house of the "King of Messengers,"
the courtyard with its single verdant tree with blessed roots.[230]

Even if enemies have seized that tree by those very roots,
God has scattered its seeds to every frontier on earth.[231]

In the midst of the mountain, a hundred kinds of trees
have raised their noble heads from its heart of soil and stone,

each tree more verdant and luxuriant than the other,
each one unfurled like flags of different nations.

So it is from one end to the other that Carmel has become
a tabernacle of the unity of all humankind.

Such a strange and glorious mystery, this wondrous garden,
extending from the mountain's height to the valley below –

reds, yellows, greens, blues and violets –
whatever the heart can conceive in color and design,

bridges fashioned from flowers and grass
connecting earth to the heavens.

Truly here every divine attribute is unveiled!
Truly this is an ensign of the eternal gardens of God!

Behold the exquisite work of the crafty sculptor –
where did he find such a flock of eagles,

these mighty birds with swift wings and keen eyes
who bear witness to this scene of greatness and glory?

These eagles encircling the gardens, come from
every corner of the earth, are gaily joined in singing,

intoning the verses as if in reverent worship.
The mountain and valley are vibrant with their voices.

There is nothing to fear from these eagles of stone;
this is not a place for birds of prey to fight.

And when in time the night arrives in its pitch black robe,
there will be more light than at any time of day,

a myriad lights brightening the mountain of Carmel,
making it shine with brilliance like a galaxy of stars

such that the heart of whoever sees this blessed site
will never forget the bleak darkness of the Máh-Kú fortress,[232]

that endless dark, that eternal silence of the stark prison,
the likes of which the world has neither seen nor heard,

which now remembered, makes tears well up in our eyes,
glistening, reflecting the lights of the terraces of Carmel.

(48) ABHÁ[223]
ANONYMOUS

O Bahá'u'lláh, may my life be a sacrifice for You,
for the light of God shines from Your soul.

Because You became manifest in the land of Iran,
its glory and majesty will emerge only from Your station.

Would that You could witness these ignorant ones,
what they have done with Your precious Iran.

But because You followed the command of God,
everyone in time will accept Your guidance.

What You accomplished is so astounding
that all who have witnessed it will become amazed by You.

For any soul who cares ought for the course of religion,
the one redress is naught but the remedy of Your medicine.

For though I myself be not a Bahá'í,
I know in my heart of hearts the worthiness of Your Cause.

The only deliverance from our affliction
is for our hands to clutch the hem of Your robe.

(49) GREETINGS AND SALUTATIONS, O ÍRÁN[234]
BY AQDAS TAWFÍQ (TÚSKÍ)

Greetings, O land of the Beloved of the world!
Greetings, O land of both despondency and joy!

Greetings, O birth place of leonine men,
O nation revered through the splendor of God!

Greetings, O charming city of Shíráz[235] –
from you did a Treasure of Mystery appear!

Greetings to you, O blessed city of Isfahán –
to your beauty of "half of the world"[236] –

for sleeping within your precincts are two pure souls:
no one has ever witnessed a sacrifice like theirs.[237]

Now only their mortal remains sleep in the soil
while their spirits soar in their celestial abode.

Greetings to the soil of Tabríz, sanctified by
the sacred blood of Rabb-i-A'lá,[238] now strewn with flowers.

I offer greetings to your glorious Yazd and to
the sacrifices made on the soil of your precincts.

My greetings to each and every town of Iran
and to the favored souls of those martyrs,

to your city of Tihrán where thousands of sweet souls,
with breasts eager and freed from all hatred,

breasts imbued with affection and the love of Abhá,
breasts that became porous from enemy bullets.

My Greetings to the assemblage of your believers,
to your noble and trustworthy youth

who have sacrificed their sweet lives
in the path of the "Intended One"[239] of the earthly realm.

It is fitting that your land become prosperous since you are
the pride of a world made felicitous by your presence.

(50) Reunion with the Beloved[240]
by Hushmand Fatheazam

Elegantly trailing His robe, He departed, leaving no trace[241] behind,
like a pleasant breeze that blows by, then instantly is gone.

He sent to the world a lightning glance from His eyes
that set ablaze a fire from which no heart was immune.

I hastened eagerly to sacrifice my life in His path;
my life was offered up, but, there was no life-taker there.

Uselessly I wept beside the rosebush of hope –
what good were flowing tears without the flowing Cypress?[242]

I pleaded, "Perhaps I could but seize the hem of Your robe!"
"Depart!" said the Beloved, "Depart, for you possess no such craft!"

Certainly a drowned ant cannot make its way out of the sea,
nor can a wounded bird fly to the heights of that sublime nest.

Nearness to the Friend requires both search and merit.
It is my salty luck[206] that I possess one but lack the other.

Unless I be a particle of dust that settles on His robe,
there is no way apparent for my reunion with Him.

Thus, I will become dust in His path, and the Beloved will pass by,
that traceless Friend so unlike any other in the world.

O my heart, glad tidings be unto you! Reunion with the Friend
is not at all remote from the beneficence of that Kind One!

Works Cited

'Abdí, Baháu'd-Dín Muhammad. *Gulzár-i-'Ishq*. Langenhain, Germany: Bahá'í Verlag, 1989.

'Abdu'l-Bahá. *Selections from the Writings of 'Abdu'l-Bahá*. Translated by Marzieh Gail et al. Haifa, Israel: Bahá'í World Centre, 1978.

'Abdu'l-Bahá. *Tablets of 'Abdu'l-Bahá*. Bahá'í Publihing Committee, 1909. (available online: http://reference.bahai.org/en/t/ab/TAB/)

The American Heritage Dictionary. 2nd College ed. Boston, MA, U.S.A.: Houghton Mifflin Co., 1985.

'Andalíb. Toronto, ON, Canada: National Spiritual Assembly of Bahá'ís of Canada (refer to the notes for specific issues).

Baalbaki, Dr. Rohi. *Al-Mawrid: A Modern Arabic-English Dictionary*. 9th ed. Beirut, Lebanon: Dar-el-Ilm Lilmalayin, 1997.

The Báb. *Selections from the Writings of the Báb*. Compiled by the Research Department of the Universal House of Justice. Translated by Habib Taherzadeh et al. Haifa, Israel: Bahá'í World Centre, 1976.

The Bahá'í International Community. *The Bahá'í Question*. New York, NY, U.S.A.: Bahá'í International Community, 1999.

Bahá'í Prayers: A Selection of Prayers Revealed by Bahá'u'lláh, the Báb, and 'Abdu'l-Bahá. Wilmette, IL, U.S.A.: Bahá'í Publishing Trust, 1991.

Bahá'u'lláh. *Gleanings from the Writings of Bahá'u'lláh*. 2nd ed. Translated by Shoghi Effendi. Wilmette, IL, U.S.A.: Bahá'í Publishing Trust, 1971.

Bahá'u'lláh. *The Hidden Words*. Translated by Shoghi Effendi. Wilmette, IL, U.S.A.: Bahá'í Publishing Trust, 1939.

Bahá'u'lláh. *The Kitáb-i-Aqdas: The Most Holy Book*. Translated by the Universal House of Justice. Haifa, Israel: Bahá'í World Centre, 1993.

Bahá'u'lláh. *The Kitáb-i-Iqán: The Book of Certitude*. 2nd ed. Translated by Shoghi Effendi. Wilmette, IL, U.S.A.: Bahá'í Publishing Trust, 1950.

Bahá'u'lláh. *The Seven Valleys and the Four Valleys*. Translated by Marzieh Gail in consultation with Ali-Kuli Khan. Wilmette, IL, U.S.A.: Bahá'í Publishing Trust, 1991.

Bahíyyih Khánum: The Greatest Holy Leaf. Compiled by the Research Department of the Universal House of Justice. Haifa, Israel: Bahá'í World Centre, 1982.

Balyuzi, H. M. *Eminent Bahá'ís in the Time of Bahá'u'lláh: With Some Historical Background*. Oxford, England: George Ronald, 1985.

Dihkhudá, 'Alí Akbar. *Lughat-Námih 'Alí Akbar Dihkhudá*. (50 Volumes). Tihrán, Írán: Tihrán University Press, 1337 Shamsí.

Ghadímí, Ríáz K. *Ríádu'l-Lughát (Arabic-Persian Dictionary)*. (6 Volumes). Toronto, ON, Canada: University of Toronto Press, 1994-2002.

Hakímíyán, 'Azíz. *Zabán-i-Dívárhá: Majmú'iy-i-Ash'ár-i-Kuhnih va Naw, 'Ishqí, Ijtimá'í, Intiqádí, Fukáhí*.

Hayyim, S. *The Larger Persian-English Dictionary*. (2 Volumes). Tihrán, Írán: Farhang-i-Mu'ásir Press, 1985.

Hornby, Helen. *Lights of Guidance: A Bahá'í Reference File*. 2d ed. New Delhi, India: Bahá'í Publishing Trust, 1988.

Khúshihá'í Az Kharman-i-Adab va Hunar. Vol. 5. Proceedings of the Society for Persian Arts and Letters, Landegg Academy. Darmstadt, Germany: Asr-i-Jadíd Publisher, 1994.

Má'idih-i-Ásmání. Compiled by Ishráq-Khávarí, 'Abdu'l-Hamíd. Tihrán, Irán: Mu'asisih-i-Matbú'át-i-Amrí, reproduced by the Bahá'í Publishing Trust of India, New Delhi, India: 1984.

Maulana, Muhammad Ali. *The Holy Qur'án, Arabic Text, English translation and Commentary*. Columbus, OH, U.S.A.: Ahmadiyyah Anjuman Isha'at Islam, Lahore, Inc., 1995.

Momen, Wendi. *Basic Bahá'í Dictionary*. Oxford, England: George Ronald, 1989.

Muhammad. *The Koran*. Translated by J. M. Rodwell. New York, NY, U.S.A.: Ballantine Books, 1993.

Muhammad. *The Holy Qur'án*. Translated by Yusif Ali. New York, NY, U.S.A.: Tahrike Tarsile Qurán Inc., 2001.

Mu'ín, Mohammad. *An Intermediate Persian Dictionary*. (6 Volumes). Tihrán, Írán: Amír Kabír Publishing Corporation, 1996.

Naghmiháy-i-Varqá. Compiled by Jabbárí, Bihrúz. Dunas, ON, Canada: Association for Bahá'í Studies in Persian, 1998.

Nabíl Zarandí. *The Dawn-Breakers: Nabíl's Narrative of the Early Days of the Bahá'í Revelation*. Translated and edited by Shoghi Effendi. Wilmette, IL, U.S.A.: Bahá'í Publishing Trust,1962.

Nabíl Zarandí. *Mathnaví-i-Nabíl-i-Zarandí*. Langenhain, Germany: Bahá'í Verlag, 1995.

Na'ím Isfahání. *Ahsanu't-Taqvím Yá Gulzár-i-Na'ím*. New Delhi, India: Shobha Printers, a reprint of the original publication in New Delhi, India, by the Bahá'í Publishing Trust of India, 1961.

Núrbakhsh, Javád. *The Núrbakhsh Treasury of Súfí Terms (Farhang-i-Núrbakhsh)*, Third printing. Tihrán, Írán: Chápkhánih-i-Marví.

Payám-i-Bahá'í. Paris, France: Assemblée Spirituélle Nationale des Bahá'ís de France (refer to footnotes for specific issues).

Payám-i-Badí'. No. 34, Vol. 3. New York, NY, U.S.A.: The Spiritual Assembly of the Bahá'ís of the City of New York, October 1985.

Rawhání, Fakhru'd-Dín Húshang. *Shahádat va Shahámat*. 1983.

Shoghi Effendi. *God Passes By*. Wilmette, IL, U.S.A.: Bahá'í Publishing Trust, 1974.

Shoghi Effendi. *The Unfolding Destiny of the British Bahá'í Community: Messages from the Guardian of the Bahá'í Faith to the Bahá'ís of the British Isles*. London, England: Bahá'í Publishing Trust, 1981.

Sulaymání, 'Azízu'lláh. *Masábíh-i-Hidáyat*. Vol. 1. Tihrán, Írán: Bahá'í Publishing Trust, 1948.

Taherzadeh, Adib. *The Revelation of Bahá'u'lláh*. (4 Volumes). Oxford, England: George Ronald, 1974-1987.

Táríkh-i-Shuhadáy-i-Yazd. Cairo, Egypt: 1347 A.H.. Reprinted by Bahá'í Publishing Trust, Pakistan, 1979.

NOTES

1. Besides the allusion in the epigram by The Greatest Holy Leaf, the "tavern" image is found is much of the mystic tradition of Persian and Arabic poetry in keeping with the entire image of drunkenness as representing being intoxicated with the love of the beloved. This comparison being in love with being intoxicated also is used in the allusions to the "cupbearer," the wine of love, and similar metaphors. The "tavern" thus symbolizes the place were the lovers assemble to celebrate the love of the Friend.

2. Quoted in *Bahiyyíh Khánum: The Greatest Holy Leaf*, compiled by the Research Department of the Universal House of Justice (Haifa, Israel: Bahá'í World Centre, 1982), p. 155.

3. 'Abdu'l-Bahá, *Selections from the Writings of 'Abdu'l-Bahá*, translated by Marzieh Gail et. al. (Haifa, Israel: Bahá'í World Centre, 1978), p. 27.

4. 'Abdu'l-Bahá, *Tablets of 'Abdu'l-Bahá* (Bahá'í Publishing Committee, 1909), p. 195. Available online at http://reference.bahai.org/en/t/ab/TAB/.

5. 'Abdu'l-Bahá, *Makátíb-i-Hadrat-i-'Abdu'l-Bahá*, vol. 2 (Cairo, Egypt: Kurdistan 'Ilmiyyah Press, 1912).

6. Ibid.

7. Ibid.

8. Mírzá Husayn of Hamadán, *The Táríkh-i-Jadíd or New History of Mírzá 'Alí Muhammad, The Báb*, translated and edited by E. G. Browne (Cambridge, England: Cambridge University Press, 1983).

9. Attributed to Sulaymán Khán.

10. Yúsuf Subhání.

11. *Khúshihá'í Az Karman-i-Adab va Hunar*, vol. 5, Proceedings of the Society for Persian Arts and Letters, Landegg Academy (Darmstadt, Germany: Asr-i-Jadíd Publisher, 1994), p. 80.

12. Bahá'u'lláh, *The Kitáb-i-Aqdas: The Most Holy Book*, translated by the Universal House of Justice (Haifa, Israel: Bahá'í World Centre, 1993), p. 20.

13. The Báb, *Selections from the Writings of the Báb*, compiled by the Research Department of the Universal House of Justice and translated by Habib Taherzadeh et. al. (Haifa, Israel: Bahá'í World Centre, 1976), p. 78.

14. 'Abdu'l-Bahá, *Makátib-i-Hadrat-i-'Abdu'l-Bahá*, p. 72.

15. Ibid.

16. *Má'idih-i-Ásmání*, compiled by 'Abdu'l-Hamíd Ishráq Khávarí (Tihrán, Írán: Mu'asisih-i-Matbú'át-i-Amrí), reproduced by the Bahá'í Publishing Trust of India, New Delhi, India, 1984, p. 73.

17. Also designated the "Apostolic" or "Primitive" age. Shoghi Effendi states that "...the Apostolic and Heroic Age of our Faith fell into three distinct epochs, of nine, of thirty-nine and of twenty-nine years duration, associated respectively with the Bábí Dispensation and the ministries of Bahá'u'lláh and of 'Abdu'l-Bahá. Helen Hornby, *Lights of Guidance: A Bahá'í Reference File*, 2nd ed. (New Delhi, India: Bahá'í Publishign Trust, 1988), p. 488.

18. The Empire from 1300-1919 of the Turks in Asia Minor, Northeast Africa, and Southeast Europe, the capital of which was Constantinople. Also known as the Turkish Empire.

19 See, for example, Nabíl Zarandí, *The Dawnbreakers: Nabíl's Narrative of the Early Days of the Bahá'í Revelation*, translated and edited by Shoghi Effendi (Wilmette, IL, U.S.A.: Bahá'í Publishing Trust, 1962), chapters 19-24, including the French footnotes.

20 *The American Heritage Dictionary*, 2nd ed. (Boston, MA, U.S.A.: Houghton Mifflin Co., 1985), p. 769.

21 Muhammad, *The Holy Qur'án*, translated by Yusif Ali (New York, NY, U.S.A.: Tahrike Tarsile Qurán Inc., 2001).

22 Ibid.

23 The word in the Qur'án is *khátam*. Bahá'u'lláh discusses the misunderstanding of this passage throughout the *Kitáb-i-Íqán*. See particularly Bahá'u'lláh, *The Kitáb-i-Íqán: The Book of Certitude*, 2nd ed., translated by Shoghi Effendi (Wilmette, IL, U.S.A.: Bahá'í Publishing Trust, 1950), pp. 162-174.

24 Bahá'u'lláh, *The Kitáb-i-Íqán*, p. 170.

25 *Pattern:* The Sunní sect of Islam take their name from the fact that, in addition to the *Sharí'at*, the laws taken both from the Qur'án and other supposedly authentic spoken guidance by the Prophet, there is guidance implicit in the pattern of life led by Muhammad Himself.

26 "He Who is everlastingly hidden from the eyes of men can never be known except through His Manifestation, and His Manifestation can adduce no greater proof of the truth of His Mission than the proof of His own Person." Bahá'u'lláh, *Gleanings from the Writings of Bahá'u'lláh*, 2nd ed., translated by Shoghi Effendi (Wilmette, IL, U.S.A.: Bahá'í Publishing Trust, 1971), p. 49.

27 Bahá'u'lláh, *The Kitáb-i-Íqán*, p. 27.

28 Bahá'u'lláh, *The Kitáb-i-Íqán*, pp. 161-162.

29 Shoghi Effendi, *God Passes By* (Wilmette, IL, U.S.A.: Bahá'í Publishing Trust, 1974), p. 217.

30 Bahá'u'lláh, *The Kitáb-i-Íqán*, p. 20.

31 Bahá'u'lláh, *Gleanings from the Writings of Bahá'u'lláh*, p. 215.

32 *The Covenant:* "Well is it with him that hath held fast unto Thy firm cord and clung to the hem of Thy resplendent robe!" Bahá'u'lláh, *Baha'i Prayers: A Selection of Prayers Revealed by Bahá'u'lláh, The Báb and 'Abdu'l-Bahá* (Wilmette, IL, U.S.A.: Bahá'í Publishing Trust, 1991), p. 164.

33 Bahá'u'lláh, *Bahá'í Prayers*, p. 213.

34 This anonymity may result from a desire to protect families in Iran, or possibly as a gesture of humility.

35 Tihrán.

36 *Chi shud:* What happened (to him)? Where is he? Whatever did befall him? Variations on this phrase are throughout the poem.

37 In one of her poems Táhiríh refers to the martyrs as "kings among kings."

38 Excerpted from Shoghi Effendi, *God Passes By*, pp. 35-42.

39 Ibid.

40 Excerpted from Nabíl Zarandí, *The Dawn-Breakers*, pp. 414-427

41 This poem is from Na'ím Isfahání, *Ahsanu't-Taqvím Yá Gulzár-i-Na'ím* (New Delhi, India: Shobha Printers), p. 195.

42   Translated from the Arabic.

43   This poem appears in *Naghmihảy-i-Varqá*, compiled by Jabbarí Bihrúz (Dundas, ON, Canada: Association for Bahá'í Studies in Persian, 1998), p. 167. Talking to Hand of the Cause Mírzá 'Alí Muhammad Varqá, Bahá'u'lláh described the power of one, like 'Abdu'l-Bahá, who possessed the transforming power of the *Elixir:* "And now, look at the Master. Observe with what patience and compassion He dealt with all types of people. He possessed this power, therefore immeasurable was the extent of the influence He would exert upon the world of humanity.

"When Varqá heard this, he was so filled with joy and excitement that he fell prostrate at Bahá'u'lláh's feet and begged Him to make it possible for him and one of his sons to lay down their lives in the path of the Master. Bahá'u'lláh favored him with His acceptance. When he returned to Persia, Varqá wrote to Bahá'u'lláh and renewed his plea for martyrdom, a plea to which He again favorably responded.

"And so it was that after many persecutions and examinations by authorities, Varqá and his twelve-year-old son Rúhu'lláh were arrested, imprisoned for the last time: "They were transferred from prison to prison weighed down with chains, their feet placed in stocks. As a result they suffered much hardship and torture until at the end Varqá was martyred when in a rage Hájibu'd-Dawlih, the chief steward in charge of the Prison of Tihrán, pierced his stomach with a dagger. Rúhu'lláh saw his father fall to the ground, and then his body was cut into pieces. A short while later, refusing to recant his faith and earnestly wishing to join his father, that noble and heroic child was strangled to death. This was in May 1896. Thus ended the life of two immortal heroes of the Bahá'í Dispensation. Both father and son have immeasurably enriched the annals of the Faith and shed such a lustre upon it that generations yet unborn will be inspired by the example of their lives and moved to scale the lofty heights of service in the promotion of the Cause of God." From Adib Taherzadeh, *The Revelation of Bahá'u'lláh*, vol. 4 (Oxford, England: George Ronald, 1987), p. 57.

This magnificent poem is a series of admonitions and axiomatic statements about how the true believer or true seeker must recognize the source of advancement if he or she is to travel the right path and serve humankind as a Bahá'í. In a letter Varqá describes the analogy of nudity and clothing in the Writings at length. He states that old and outworn beliefs are like an old garment. One should take this old garment off and swim in the limitless ocean of the Revelation. The old garment symbolizes the sciences, laws, and vain imaginations fabricated by the ordinary human beings. The divine garment, however, never ages.

44   "Am I not your Lord?" This phrase relates to the story of creation. The Covenant of God with humankind at the dawn of creation occurs when man responds with "Yes, Yes" to His call of "Am I not your Lord?"

45   *Mahram:* One who has permission to enter the shrine or inner sanctum. One who possesses great knowledge.

46   The sense here is that because you potentially manifest divine attributes, to know your true self is to appreciate the divine attributes with which you have been invested. A more direct parallel is Bahá'u'lláh's statement in the *Kitáb-i-Íqán*, p. 101, that we come to know God by knowing our self: "For in him are potentially revealed all the attributes and names of God to a degree that no other created being hath excelled or surpassed. All these names and attributes are applicable to him. Even as He hath said: 'Man is My mystery, and I am his mystery'."

47   Literally, "O He!" a term uttered by the Dervishes calling out to God.

48   One whose prayers are answered; one who is spiritual.

49 The *pearl* could refer to the poem or to the poet's soul.

50 *Dam:* In Súfí terminology, "The breath of the Merciful (God)" and the breath of the "Perfect Man" that heals (like the breath of Jesus), speech, speaking, a poem, the rhythm of poetry.

51 As in the controversial Qur'ánic verse stating that Muhammad is the *seal* of the Prophets, the word used here is *khátam*, a seal that is used to mean that the letter is completed.

52 In your selflessness or in the state of attaining "true poverty and absolute nothingness."

53 Jam is the title of an ancient king of Persia who established Naw Rúz as a festival day. According to the legend, he owned a "world displaying cup" by means of which one could see the entire universe and all the good and bad things happening in it.

54 This poem is from *Naghmiháy-i-Varqá*, pp. 318-319.

55 *The Holy Qur'án*, 7:23.

56 Abraham.

57 Nimrod wanted Abraham to be killed in the fire he had prepared, but according to legend, the fire turned into a flower garden. The actual verses in the The Holy Qur'án, 21:68, merely mention that Abraham commanded the fire to be cool, not that it turned into a flower garden. However, poetically, a fire with its beautiful colors of cool would have the appearance of a flower garden.

58 Moses. Interestingly, the allusion to "Your fire" would seem to be a reference to God, but in the authoritative Bahá'í texts is a statement that it is the voice of Bahá'u'lláh that speaks to Moses from the burning bush: "Bahá'u'lláh is not the intermediary between other Manifestations and God. Each has His own relation to the Primal Source. But in the sense that Bahá'u'lláh is the greatest Manifestation to yet appear, the One who consummates the Revelation of Moses, He was the One Moses conversed with in the Burning Bush. In other words, Bahá'u'lláh identifies the glory of the God-Head on that occasion with Himself. No distinction can be made amongst the Prophets in the sense that They all proceed from one Source, and are of one essence. But Their stations and functions in this world are different." From Shoghi Effendi, *The Unfolding Destiny of the British Bahá'í Community: Messages from the Guardian of the Bahá'í Faith to the Bahá'ís of the British Isles* (Lodnon, England: Bahá'í Publishing Trust, 1981), p. 448.

59 Job.

60 Mi'ráj refers to "The Ascent of Muhammad, the mystic vision of His night journey in which He was transported from Mecca to Jerusalem and shown the signs of God." From Wendi Momen, ed., *A Basic Bahá'í Dictionary* (Oxford, England: George Ronald, 1989), p. 157.

61 Also "brave,"" pious," or "wise."

62 The dwellers of both heaven and earth. In Muslim mythology a jinee is a spirit that can appear as a human or animal.

63 It is laden with sadness.

64 This poem is from *Naghmiháy-i-Varqá*, p. 64. The title of this poem is probably given to the piece by the editor of the Persian text, not by Varqá himself since it was uncommon at the time for Persian poets to title their works. Similar to the poetry of Táhirih, this poem is highly complex and allusive. Its simple expressions totally belie the depth of thought to which the poet refers. Clearly the poet writes this verse not primarily for the common reader, but for the learned who would be capable of discerning the subtle character of this poem.

To the religious and the pious, the detail of the obligatory prayer rituals are very important. The clergy admonished and advised the faithful not to miss the ablutions or any other details. The mystics, however, pay attention primarily to the purity of heart and the demonstration of sincere devotion to the Beloved. Furthermore, the mystics accuse the pretentious advisors of hypocrisy.

We have taken the liberty here of transforming the couplets into quatrains because of the line length and also because there are in most lines two component ideas, as is common among other classical uses of couplets in Persian poetry.

65 As opposed to water.

66 Traditional Gnostic poetic image of the eyebrows of the Beloved which attract the poor lover by their beauty and entrap him, as does the image of the black hair which indicates the tests and difficulties of the world of existence, the material world of multiplicity, in contrast to the spiritual world of the Absolute.

67 Here the implication would seem to be that the speaker does not know whether to adore God according to the evidences of God's perfection as manifest in the particular expressions of beauty in the world of creation, or simply to use the more encompassing notion of loving God a priori because God will never do aught but that which is just, right, or appropriate.

68 Published in *Payám-i-Bahá'í*, no. 204 (Paris, France: Assemblée Spirituelle Nationale des Bahá'í de France), p. 26.

69 Another metaphor is the story of Dhu'l-Qarnayn, who with Khidr, the prophet, set out to search for the water of life. The water of life is found in the darkness. Therefore, they left the inhabited world, entering the darkness that lies behind it. Dhu'l-Qarnayn means "the one with two horns," and is an indication of power and authority. In ancient mythology and history, important people such as Alexander the Great have been given this title. In the Qur'án, in response to the questions asked from Muhammad, the story of the Dhu'l-Qarnayn is mentioned. Dhu'l-Qarnayn reached where the sun sets. The sun was going down in muddy water. 'Abdu'l-Bahá explains the esoteric meaning of the Qur'ánic verses on Dhu'l-Qarnayn and the reason why this story, as is, was revealed in the Qur'án:

"But the verses related to Dhu'l-Qarnayn are the esoteric verses (*mutashábihát*). They have interpretations. The opposers (to Muhammad) asked the question so that perhaps an answer would be produced which was against their beliefs and this would cause hesitations among the believers. Therefore, Dhu'l-Qarnayn's case was seemingly revealed according to the beliefs of the opposers, so that they could not contend. However, in each word of it there is a mystery. Dhu'l-Qarnayn here refers to His Holiness Amír, who, through his heart, searched all the world and investigated the Universal Manifestation (*mazhar-i-kullí*). He observed that the sun of reality is hidden in the frame of water and earth." (Provisional translation from *Má'idih-i-Ásmání*, Part II, p. 43.)

'Abdu'l-Bahá in the above passage explains that the spiritual and Divine reality appears in the frame (body and mold) of earthly and dark creation (the muddy water). This is the phenomena of the manifestation of God's names and attributes in the corporal world of creation, which is called the Universal Manifestation. The water of life also alludes to the mystery of immortality. Immortality of the soul can be achieved through one's search and struggle in this dark and perishable material existence. This is the purpose of physical reality.

70 Taken from *'Andalíb*, vol. 9, no. 35, summer 1990 (Toronto, ON, Canada: National Spiritual Assembly of the Bahá'ís of Canada) p. 56, this famous poem is by Liqá'í Káshání. Each couplet ends with the phrase mazi dárad, "it's heavenly" or "is heavenly." Literally the phrase means "it is tasty," but the connotative meaning is something like "you'd love it," "you should see it," "it's lovely," "it's fun,"

or "it's an experience you don't want to miss," etc. At times it is used ironically, as when alluding to pain and suffering.

71 An expression meaning that the speaker has suffered and is on the verge of death.

72 The source of this poem is *Naghmihày-i-Varqá*.

73 This is the only extant poem from the hand of Rúhu'lláh, who at age twelve was martyred with his father Varqá in May of 1896. It is composed in the form of a Sáqí-Námih, a genre in the Mathnaví form in which the speaker asks for wine from the "cupbearer" to help overcome his sorrow. In this poem, the sorrow results from the speaker's desire to escape the bonds of mortal existence and to ascend to the spiritual realm. It employs the same meter used by Rúmí and Bahá'u'lláh in their respective mathnavís, a meter called *Bahr-i-Máhdhúf*.

Though traditional and ostensibly imitative in some respects, the end result of Rúhu'lláh's verse is a thoroughly complex structure whereby instead of simply alluding to his fidelity before the Covenant of Bahá'u'lláh, he actually structures the poem so as to elucidate the properties of the Covenant as he pays homage first to Bahá'u'lláh and then to 'Abdu'l-Bahá.

That a believer at age twelve could comprehend these concepts in such depth, let alone articulate them in such eloquent verse, is indeed astounding.

74 *Paran* is the desert in which the Israelites wandered. The blaze refers to the fire Moses witnessed emanating from the burning bush.

75 'Abdu'l-Bahá was appointed Center of the Covenant in Bahá'u'lláh's will, but took the name 'Abdu'l-Bahá *(Servant of Bahá)* to counteract the accusations of Covenant-Breakers that He was claiming to be a Manifestation. 'Abdu'l-Bahá made many powerful statements to the effect that His sole purpose in life was servitude to Bahá'u'lláh.

76 *Áthár:* "vestiges," a term used in Bahá'í Writings to allude to the authoritative texts; 'Abdu'l-Bahá was conferred by Bahá'u'lláh to have the power of authoritative interpretation of the revealed words of Bahá'u'lláh.

77 *Alif:* The first letter of the alphabet written as a straight vertical line. Alif is composed of points and therefore can be said to be generated through the movement of the point. Alif itself, however, is considered to be the source and root of the second letter of the alphabet, bá, as well as the other letters. Thus, alif has been used in Persian literature as an allusion to the "source" or the "beginning" of something: e.g., the First Mind, the first creation of God; single, pure, detached and free; beautifully erect and tall, like the figure of the beloved.

78 In contrast to *alif*, *bá* is written as a horizontal line with a dot under it. The poet uses this letter as a symbol of lowliness. Perhaps he is alluding to the fact that the Báb, whose name starts with *bá*, comes as a Herald for Bahá'u'lláh. But here he is most likely referring to the fact that 'Abdu'l-Bahá humbled Himself (prostrate like *bá*) before Bahá'u'lláh.

79 *Rawdih:* "Garden" or "grave" here refers to the burial place of Bahá'u'lláh *(Rawdih-i-Mubárakih)*.

80 An allusion to 'Abdu'l-Bahá probably taken from a passage in Bahá'u'lláh, *Kitáb-i-Aqdas*, p. 63: "When the ocean of My presence hath ebbed and the Book of My Revelation is ended, turn your faces toward Him Whom God hath purposed, Who hath branched from this Ancient Root."

81 This is a provisional translation of a verse from a prayer in the form of a mathnaví by 'Abdu'l-Bahá.

82 This is the story of Varqá and his son Rúhu'lláh. It also addresses extensive massacres that took place at that time because of the murder of Násiri'd-Dín Sháh. Bahá'ud-Dín Muhammad 'Abdí,

Gulzár-i-'Ishq (Langenhein, Germany: Bahá'í Verlag, 1989), pp. 98-102. In H. M. Balyuzi, *Eminent Bahá'í's in the Time of Bahá'u'lláh: With some Historical Background* (Oxford, England: George Ronald, 1985), p. 96:

"Brought face to face with Varqá in that inner room, Hájibu'd-Dawlih had gone immediately into a fierce tirade: 'You did at last what you did,' he had shouted at Varqá, to which the poet had quietly answered that he was unaware of having done anything wrong. Varqá's calm reply had added to the fury of Hájibu'd-Dawlih. It had indeed maddened him. Dragging his dagger out of its sheath, he had plunged it into the chest of Varqá, saying with great relish: 'How are you?' And Varqá had answered him thus: 'Feeling better than you.' 'Tell me,' said Hájibu'd-Dawlih, 'which one shall I slay first, you, or your son?' And quietly Varqá had replied, 'It is the same to me.' Then, having torn open Varqá's chest, Hájibud-Dawlih had handed him over to his executioners, whereupon four of them had fallen on the poet, tearing him apart, limb from limb. As his blood kept flowing in profusion, Rúhu'lláh was crying out: 'O dear father, father dear, take me, take me, take me with you.'

"Having destroyed Varqá, the unspeakable Hájibud-Dawlih had turned to Rúhu'lláh, who had just witnessed the dismemberment and slaughter of his father: 'Do not weep. I shall take you with myself, make you an allowance, obtain for you a post from the Sháh.' And bravely, Rúhu'lláh had replied: 'I do not want you. I do not want your allowance. I do not want any post that you might obtain for me. I want to join my father.' Then, he had begun weeping afresh. Defied, baulked, repelled, Hájibu'd-Dawlih had ordered his minions to bring a rope and strangle that brave boy. No rope was available there, and so they had put Rúhu'lláh's neck in the loop of the instrument of the bastinado. When he had become still, they had dropped the senseless corpse on the floor."

83 The double entendre here is that the word bower can mean literally a tree branch or a bridal chamber, a bedroom.

84 The male bird feels he has been insensitive, and his mate's words make him feel guilty.

85 A reference to Hájibud-Dawlih.

86 Another double entendre is created here in that the title Varqá means *dove*. Thus we have a female bird, possibly a dove, speak of the "Dove of Paradise."

87 This frequently used metaphor has the feel of appellations used in various ethnic cultures where people are given names of animals or objects that befit their attributes. The "walking cypress" implies one (usually a male) who is stalwart, beautiful, graceful, and lordly in comportment.

88 He is speaking to his own soul.

89 The Day of Resurrection.

90 "It was the mother of this same Ashraf who, when sent to the prison in the hope that she would persuade her only son to recant, had warned him that she would disown him were he to denounce his faith, had bidden him follow the example of Abá-Basír, and had even watched him expire with eyes undimmed with tears." (Shoghi Effendi, *God Passes By*, p. 199).

91 As the two birds (narrators) joined the other birds to tell them the story of Varqá.

92 This poem is from 'Azízu'lláh Sulaymání, *Masábíh-i-Hidáyat*, vol. 1 (Tihrán, Írán: Bahá'í Publishing Trust, 1948), pp. 331-333. This poem is a marthyih or elegy eulogizing Varqá and Rúhu'lláh. Many marthyihs have been written for the martyrs of Karbilá and for the Imám Hussein, and many are chanted from the pulpit during the month of mourning (Muharram) while the audience weeps and laments.

Like the grief and deeply emotional lamentation of a mother who has lost a child, this genre of poem is simple but rhythmic and deeply penetrating. Indeed, 'Abdu'l-Bahá wrote a letter to Nayyir and Síná praising them for writing such a great marthyih for the occasion of the martyrdom of this father and son. After admiring the literary and poetic merits of the piece, he ends the letter by stating, "The reward of this poem shall be determined in the 'Abhá kingdom." [provisional translation].

While the original is in the traditional form of couplets, we have broken the lines into quatrains because this does a better job of capturing the pace, meter, and feel of the original.

93 Tihrán.

94 Chi shud: What happened (to him)? Where is he? What ever did befall him? Variations on this phrase are throughout the poem.

95 The soft blowing wind from the East. In the story of Solomon, the wind, which was his obedient servant, used to take the news of all that happened across his kingdom to him. Therefore the wind is the bearer of news.

96 The title Varqá meaning "dove" was given to the distinguished poet, 'Alí-Muhammad, by Bahá'u'lláh.

97 The legendary bird living on the mountain of Qáf. In Gnostic terminology, the *Símurgh* is a symbol of a mystical station as in *Conference of the Birds* by Attár.

98 Both metaphors of the *chick* and the *fawn* allude to Rúhu'lláh as the offspring of Varqá.

99 *Há* is the Arabic letter with which the word *Hová* (God) starts. Therefore the desert of *Há* should mean the Divine plain or the Divine realm.

100 Varqá and Rúhu'lláh were both scholars and eloquent speakers. The rulers who would arrange for their debates with the clergy and with the rest of the audience used to enjoy and admire their knowledge and eloquence. Normally, after Varqá used to end his speech, he would then ask his young son to deliver a speech. At times meetings were arranged, and many, including high ranking officials, would attend just to admire and enjoy the sweetness and eloquence of Rúhu'lláh's utterance.

101 We have taken some liberties with these lines, but this is the sense of the original.

102 According to *The Holy Qur'án*, 21:69, Abraham walked in the fire which his enemies had set up to kill him, but the fire turned cold and Abraham was saved. This is probably an allusion to that event.

103 In the Qur'án the story of the discovery of Joseph by a passing caravan is described as follows:

"Then there came a caravan of travelers: they sent their water-carrier (for water), and he let down his bucket (into the well)... He said: 'Ah there! Good news! Here is a (fine) young man!' So they concealed him as a treasure! But Allah knoweth well all that they do!" (*The Holy Qur'án,* 12:19).

According to the Rodwell translation, the story is as follows:

"And wayfarers came and sent their drawer of water, and he let down his bucket. 'Good news!' said he, 'This is a youth!' And they kept his case secret, to make merchandise of him. But God knew what they did." (The Koran, translated by J. M. Rodwell (New York, NY, U.S.A.: Ballantine Books, 1993), 12: Joseph, Peace be on Him).

104 This is an important analogy in Rumi's work. The reed flute pours forth elegiac tones because it laments its separation from the weed bed, even as the lover laments separation from the Beloved Friend.

105 Nabíl, the Bahá'í historian, composed a Mathnaví in which he describes the history of the Faith. This poem is an example of his Mathnaví describing the events related to the martyrdom of Hájí

Mullá Hasan, Zayn'ul-Muqarrabín's cousin. The original is taken from Nabíl Zarandí, *Mathnaví-i-Nabíl-i-Zarandí* (Langenhain, Germany: Bahá'í Verlag, 1995), pp. 45-46. Lacking much imagery or detail (other than the dream), this work is more of a story than a poem, as would be appropriate to a chronicler like Nabíl, but the work is worthwhile because it, too, demonstrates that while many sacrificed their lives rather than recant their Faith, it was not a simple or painless choice, nor was it a reflexive decision derived from any sort of mindless fanaticism with which many presently associate the concept of "martyrdom."

106 Though he drowned himself because he was unable to endure the death of Bahá'u'lláh, his life was an emblem of devotion.

107 Literally, "your name has been entered in the book of soldiers." *Sarbáz* here means one who gambles his head and has a literary connotation of one who loses (sacrifices, offers, risks) his life.

108 This passage can be taken to mean that the Manifestation has the power to do whatsoever He wills in regard to the events surrounding His Cause.

109 This poem is from *Ahsanu't-Taqvím Yá Gulzár-i-Na'ím*, p. 247.

110 This alludes to two famous love stories often cited in Persian literature: the story of Shírín and Farhád, and that of Laylí and Majnún. They are archetypal lovers much as are Romeo and Juliet in Western literature.

111 This is the sort of paradox or enigma alluded to in the introductory note wherein external or macrocosmic order is reversed and/or disordered because of the impact of the love between the lover and the beloved. In this case, of course, the order of the world as it has been is quite literally reversed by the advent of the Prophet who, in bringing about true justice, totally destroys what has been constructed in the guise of justice by those who seek power and position.

112 The last couplet is in Arabic in the form of a prayer and an expression of wonderment.

113 This poem is from *Ahsanu't-Taqvím Yá Gulzár-i-Na'ím*, p. 246, and focuses on the irony of those who eagerly give up their lives rather than recant their belief in Bahá'u'lláh.

114 "The House of Peace," a title for the city of Baghdád. The verse itself refers to the following story: "From such a treasury of precious memories it will suffice my purpose to cite but a single instance, that of one of His ardent lovers, a native of Zavárih, Siyyid Ismá'íl by name, surnamed Dhabíh (the sacrifice), formerly a noted divine, taciturn, meditative and wholly severed from every earthly tie, whose self-appointed task, on which he prided himself, was to sweep the approaches of the house in which Bahá'u'lláh was dwelling. Unwinding his green turban, the ensign of his holy lineage, from his head, he would, at the hour of dawn, gather up, with infinite patience, the rubble which the footsteps of his Beloved had trodden, would blow the dust from the crannies of the wall adjacent to the door of that house, would collect the sweepings in the folds of his own cloak, and, scorning to cast his burden for the feet of others to tread upon, would carry it as far as the banks of the river and throw it into its waters. Unable, at length, to contain the ocean of love that surged within his soul, he, after having denied himself for forty days both sleep and sustenance, and rendering for the last time the service so dear to his heart, betook himself, one day, to the banks of the river, on the road to Kázimayn, performed his ablutions, lay down on his back, with his face turned towards Baghdád, severed his throat with a razor, laid the razor upon his breast, and expired." From Shoghi Effendi, *God Passes By*, p. 136.

115 An allusion to the story of Badí', who carried a tablet on foot from Bahá'u'lláh to Násiru'd-Dín Sháh, knowing he would be executed when the king read the tablet.

116 "Abá-Basír and Siyyid Ashraf, whose fathers had been slain in the struggle of Zanján, were decapitated on the same day in that city, the former going so far as to instruct, while kneeling in prayer, his executioner as to how best to deal his blow, while the latter, after having been so brutally beaten that blood flowed from under his nails, was beheaded, as he held in his arms the body of his martyred companion." From Shoghi Effendi, God Passes By, p. 199.

117 Italics here and elsewhere indicate the passage is in Arabic.

118 Na'ím is here referring to the martyrdom of Áqá Mullá 'Alí of Sabzivár, one of the seven martyrs of Yazd. In the History of the Martyrs of Yazd a description of this grievous event is provided. They chained all seven together. They released the one at the beginning of the chain, martyred him and proceeded to another part of town with drums and trumpets playing and the crowd participating in stoning or in some creative way disgracing the corpse that was not yet completely lifeless and still moving. The Jews were forced to drag the bodies from one place to another. The last verse of this poem is a paraphrase of what Áqá Mullá 'Alí of Sabzivár proclaimed at the moment of his martyrdom: "When they arrived by the gate of the Mosque of Mírzá 'Abdu'l-Karím, at the three-way junction, close to the house of Shaykh Muhammad Hasan, they took the chain off his holiness Áqá Mullá 'Alí of Sabzivár to martyr him. Mubárak Khán addressed his holiness and said, "I pity for you since you are a stranger. Just say one word of aversion and I will not let them kill you and I will buy your blood for three hundred Túmáns from His Eminence (the prince-governor)." At this time, the executioner had taken a knife in his hand and was standing ready and waiting so that maybe he would utter a word of aversion, and all the people were silent and quiet, absorbed and dumbfounded all looking at his holiness. And the drum and the trumpet were quiet, and you could not hear one's breathing. His holiness, with a loud voice that all people could hear said, "In the desert of Karbilá, His Holiness the Prince of Martyrs (Imám Hussayn) uttered: 'Is there a helper to help me?' and I, humbly say: 'Is there a witness to witness me?' He said this in a way that all people heard and then Afrásyáb, the executioner pulled his knife out to cut his head off. His holiness, personally raised his head, while standing, cut his own holy throat and threw away. And they took the other three holy persons, with drums and trumpet and clarion and set out. Later on, a farmer fellow arrived with his spade in his hand. He segmented that holy corpse with the tip of his spade, joint by joint, and they set that torn apart corpse on fire. And his honor's age was around forty-five. (Translated from *Tárikh-i-Shuhadáy-i-Yazd* (Cairo, Egypt: 1347 A.H.), pp. 48-49). A short summary of the martyrdom of the seven martyrs of Yazd can be found in Taherzadeh, *The Revelation of Bahá'u'lláh*, vol. 4, p. 147 and in Shoghi Effendi, *God Passes By*, pp. 201-201.

119 From 'Abdí, *Gulzár-i-'Ishq*, p. 24.

120 Bahá'u'lláh calls Siyyid Muhammad of Isfahán the "one-eyed" man in the Kitáb-i-Iqán: "And yet, notwithstanding all these admonitions, We perceive that a one-eyed man, who himself is the chief of the people, is arising with the utmost malevolence against Us." (Bahá'u'lláh, *The Kitáb-i-Íqán*, p. 248) However, there are other allusions in the Bahá'í texts to a "one-eyed man": e.g., Mullá Muhammad-i-Mamaqání, "that one-eyed white-bearded renegade" (Shoghi Effendi, *God Passes By*, p. 21), and Hájí Mírzá Karím Khán (Zarandí, *The Dawn-Breakers*, p. 39).

121 This poem is from *Payám-i-Bahá'í*, No. 248, January 2000, p. 17. In this poem, the line lengths and the natural caesura make the translation of couplets into quatrains helpful to the beauty of the verse in English and to the clarity of the poem. The reader would do well to pay careful attention to the strong use of irony in this historical recounting of the martyrdom of the Báb.

122 *Humá*: A kind of eagle that eats bones. Literally it means auspicious. People used to believe that anyone who falls under the shadow of this bird will have good luck.

123 Literally *high-head*. Also means *distinct, honored*.

124 This is an allusion to the fact that after the Báb's execution, his remains were hidden and moved secretly from place to place for fifty years:

"On the evening of the very day of the Bab's execution, which fell on the ninth of July 1850 (28th of Sha'bán 1266 A.H.), during the thirty-first year of His life and the seventh of His ministry, the mangled bodies were transferred from the courtyard of the barracks to the edge of the moat outside the gate of the city. Four companies, each consisting of ten sentinels, were ordered to keep watch in turn over them. On the following morning the Russian Consul in Tabríz visited the spot, and ordered the artist who had accompanied him to make a drawing of the remains as they lay beside the moat. In the middle of the following night a follower of the Báb, Hájí Sulaymán Khán, succeeded, through the instrumentality of a certain Hájí Alláh-Yár, in removing the bodies to the silk factory owned by one of the believers of Mílán, and laid them, the next day, in a specially made wooden casket, which he later transferred to a place of safety. Meanwhile the mullas were boastfully proclaiming from the pulpits that, whereas the holy body of the Immaculate Imam would be preserved from beasts of prey and from all creeping things, this man's body had been devoured by wild animals. No sooner had the news of the transfer of the remains of the Báb and of His fellow-sufferer been communicated to Bahá'u'lláh than He ordered that same Sulaymán Khán to bring them to Tihrán, where they were taken to the Imám-Zádih-Hasan, from whence they were removed to different places, until the time when, in pursuance of 'Abdu'l-Bahá's instructions, they were transferred to the Holy Land, and were permanently and ceremoniously laid to rest by Him in a specially erected mausoleum on the slopes of Mt. Carmel." From Shoghi Effendi, *God Passes By*, p. 54.

125 "The very moment the shots were fired a gale of exceptional violence arose and swept over the city. From noon till night a whirlwind of dust obscured the light of the sun, and blinded the eyes of the people." From.Shoghi Effendi, *God Passes By*, p. 53.

126 The irony here is that it is forbidden to kill animals in the sacred sanctuary (the haram) of the kaaba in Mecca. Therefore, one is not allowed to shoot at the pigeons of the haram, but they are executing a Manifestation of God.

127 The house of the Báb in Shíráz, a sacred place of pilgrimage for Bahá'ís, was demolished.

128 *Shabdíz*: The name of a horse of Khusraw Parvíz (a king of ancient Persia). The black horse, which was brought from Rome, was taller than other horses. The name itself means "dark night."

129 A reference to the wild horse offered to the Báb in Urúmíyyih. See Shoghi Effendi, ed. and trans., *The Dawn-Breakers*, pp. 309-310.

130 The high seat with steps in front in the mosque on which mulláhs sit to preach .

131 An *adytum* is the principle place in a mosque where the Imám leads the people in prayer.

132 *Shahpar*: the largest feathers on the lead edge of a bird's wing that enables it to have lift in flight; hence, this term alludes to those figures who gave the power and spiritual upliftment to the besieged occupants of the fort.

133 This poem is typical of many of Na'ím's poems in its simple and direct language and in its ability to touch the reader's heart directly and powerfully. The source of the poem is Nai'ím Isfaháni, *Ahsan'ut-Taqvím Yá Gulzár-i-Na'ím*, p. 191. The poem is placed after his verse celebrating the arrival of 'Abdu'l-Bahá in the United States. It appears to paraphrase one of the speeches that 'Abdu'l-Bahá delivered in the West

134 The word *gawhar*, meaning jewel, seems here to allude to the Bahá'í belief that all human souls are emanations from God.

135 *Taqvím:* mould, symmetry, form, nature, constitution. See *The Holy Qur'án*, 95:4: "We have indeed created man in the best of molds." This also alludes to the same word and concept (balance, symmetry) in Genesis where man is described as being fashioned in the "image" of God.

136 This poem is from Nai'ím Isfaháni, *Ahsanu't-Taqvím Yá Gulzár-i-Na'ím*, p. 190. It was written by Na'ím, the poet-philosopher of Isfahán, on the occasion of 'Abdu'l-Bahá's arrival in the United States in 1912.

137 The allusion here is to the unity of ethnically diverse peoples. The Daylams were a brave people who resisted the conquest of the Arabs, whereas the Tajíks were reputed to be a passive and even a cowardly people. Tájík is also used to refer to an Arab who grows up among the Persians. In this sense, one might expect animosity between the Tájíks and the Daylams (who were resisting the Arabs).

138 This poem is from 'Abdí, *Gulzár-i-'Ishq*, pp. 77-78.

139 *King of the Brave Ones:* a title alluding to 'Alí, the first Imám of Shí'ih Islam and the fourth Calif of Sunni Islam.

140 *The Chosen One:* one of the titles of Muhammad.

141 Title taken from Bahá'u'lláh, *The Hidden Words*, translated by Shoghi Effendi (Wilmette, IL, U.S.A.: Bahá'í Publishing Trust, 1939), #24 from the Persian. This poem is from 'Abdí, *Gulzár-i-'Ishq*, p. 13.

142 *Masá'il* (question) refers to the religious questions often asked of the clergy. A member of the high clergy (Áyatu'lláh) normally composes a book answering such religious questions (lexicon of questions).

143 *Hadd* means *limit*, but it also alludes to religious laws and cannons.

144 This poem is from *Payám-i-Bahá'í*, no. 177, August 1994, p. 39. 'Abdu'l-Bahá interprets the phrase "the Sure Handle" as a reference in the holy texts to the Covenant of God: "The glory of God rest upon thee and upon them that hold fast unto the sure handle of His Will and holy Covenant" From 'Abdu'l-Bahá, *Selections from the Writings of 'Abdu'l-Bahá*, p. 205. We also find the term "sure Handle" and "firm Handle" being used in the same context.

145 The pain of love longing and/or the pain endured in the path of attaining the Divine Presence.

146 Muhammad, *The Holy Qur'án*, 2:256.

147 The next line in the same Qur'ánic verse states: "Now is the right way made distinct from error." From Muhammad, *The Holy Qur'án*, 2:257.

148 An allusion to the Covenant of God found in the Bahá'í scriptures and in the Qur'án.

149 This poem is from 'Abdí, *Gulzár-i-'Ishq*, p. 50-51.

150 God is alluded to as a "Hidden Treasure" in a well-known tradition by Imám 'Alí.

151 This is a very explicit allusion to the well-known tradition of the Hidden Treasure, a tradition 'Abdu'l-Bahá discusses at length. In essence, the tradition explains why God fashioned human beings, and the heart of its meaning is captured succinctly in several Hidden Words: e.g., "O SON OF MAN! I loved thy creation, hence I created thee. Wherefore, do thou love Me, that I may name thy name and fill thy soul with the spirit of life." From Bahá'u'lláh, *The Hidden Words*, #4 from the Arabic.

152 A reference to Mírzá Mihdí and his fall through the skylight in the prison at Akká. Though Bahá'u'lláh might have cured him, the boy requested that his life be accepted as a ransom for those who had been unable to attain his Father's presence.

153 Published in *Payám-i-Bahá'í*, no. 249-250, August-September 2000, p. 47.

154 "'My pen,' writes the chronicler of the bloody episodes associated with the birth and rise of our Faith, 'shrinks in horror in attempting to describe what befell those valiant men and women.... What I have attempted to recount of the horrors of the siege of Zanján ... pales before the glaring ferocity of the atrocities perpetrated a few years later in Nayríz and Shíráz.' The heads of no less than two hundred victims of these outbursts of ferocious fanaticism were impaled on bayonets, and carried triumphantly from Shíráz to Ábádih. Forty women and children were charred to a cinder by being placed in a cave, in which a vast quantity of firewood had been heaped up, soaked with naphtha and set alight. Three hundred women were forced to ride two by two on bare-backed horses all the way to Shíráz. Stripped almost naked they were led between rows of heads hewn from the lifeless bodies of their husbands, sons, fathers and brothers. Untold insults were heaped upon them, and the hardships they suffered were such that many among them perished." From Shoghi Effendi, *God Passes By*, p. 79.

155 The name bestowed by Bahá'ís on the place where the heads of the martyrs are buried in Ábádih.

156 The word is a Súfí term meaning "annihilation," but Bahá'u'lláh uses the term in his description of the seventh valley in *The Seven Valleys*.

157 This poem is taken from *Payám-i-Bahá'í*, no. 238, September 1999, p. 16. It is by an unnamed collaborator of the magazine. Each verse ends with the word imrúz, which means "today."

158 Referring to the ancient eternity: "Am I not your Lord?"

159 *Vaqfih*: a place of standing still; a pause, delay, or hesitation. This is a Súfí term meaning a pause between two stations of progress that occurs when the wayfarer has not adequately understood the station he has completed and thus does not deserve to enter into a higher station. Therefore, the wayfarer is wandering between the two stages of progress.

160 The Hegelian philosophy of history as predetermined.

161 The realm of spiritual reality.

162 *Sayrúrat*: "becoming"; a philosophical term from the philosophy of Heraclitus, the Greek philosopher who believed that the universe is subject to constant flow and flux. Therefore, one cannot say that things are, but they become. In the modern world, Alfred North Whitehead's *Process Philosophy* addresses the concept of continuous change, for even though process philosophy is as old as the 6th century BC, the Greek philosopher Heraclitus renewed interest in it.

163 From *Payám-i-Bahá'í*, no. 252, November 2000, p. 60. This poem is by Mr. Muhammad Ridá Hisámí who was jailed at the Jalál Ábád prison of Shíráz for seven years and endured immense hardship and cruelty.

164 Also: "group" or "tribe."

165 A Persian expression meaning that one must see something for himself in order to understand it.

166 The three words of "exalted," "supreme," and 'Alí (lofty) are derivations of the same root of 'Alá meaning "praised." 'Alí is the Báb's name ('Alí Muhammad). He was imprisoned in the fortress of Chihríq the last two years before His execution.

167 The title given to the prison city of 'Akká by Bahá'u'lláh on His arrival to the city.

168 *Ghusn-i-Mumtáz*, a title of Shoghi Effendi.

169 *Válá:* can also mean "dear" or "famous."

170 *Válí:* the administrator or governor; "honorable" and "Guardian" are derivations from the same root of valíya meaning "administrated."

171 By this time in the poem, the poet-martyr has transformed the meaning of "prison" to the meaning it often has in the tablets of Bahá'u'lláh – the "kingdom of names," the nether world of illusion. In short, "prison" alludes to mortality and our temporary imprisonment in it, as well as the paradox that being in prison and martyred for the Cause of God is to become truly free because of what these four figures have accomplished.

172 This poem is found in Fakhru'd-Dín Húshang Rawhání, *Shahádat va Shahámat* (1983), p. 1.

173 From Bihrúz Bihishtí, a contemporary Persian Bahá'í poet. Poem appears in *'Andalíb*, vol. 8, no. 30, spring 1989, p. 52.

174 Published in *Payám-i-Bahá'í*, no. 182, January 1995, p. 29. This is part of a poem by Sálihzádih Samarqandí, a Bahá'í from Uzbekistan who, with other friends of Uzbekistan, was exiled to Siberia and died there. He composed this poem in 1928. Here we observe the grit and determination of a martyr who refuses to give voice to any wavering or doubt, as if he is quite aware that others look to him as an example.

175 I have no need to coerce you.

176 Published in *Payám-i-Bahá'í*, no. 189, August 1995, p. 10.

177 As explained in the introduction, the term "tavern" *(maykhánih)* is a Gnostic term – the station of *Láhút* (Divinity) and Unity of Essence that has filled the cup of all determinations of existence (determinations in God's Knowledge) (Javád Núrbakhsh, *The Núrbakhsh Treasury of Súfí Terms (Farhang-i-Núrbakhsh)*, 3rd printing (Tihran, Iran: Cháp̄khánih-i-Marví), 1-160. The phrase here would imply that the speaker has recognized his Divine origin and is determined to remain in touch with her spiritual reality forever. He also contrasts the honesty of the dwellers of the Tavern with the duplicity of the pretentious pious ones.

178 Implicitly, "except clinging to the hem of your robe."

179 This is from *'Andalíb*, vol. 9, no. 35, Summer 1990, p. 56. This poem, by the recent martyr Awjí, plays off the previous poem (#17) by Liqá'í. The poem is what is called in Persian an *istiqbál* or "welcoming" – whereby he follows the same style and uses the same closing phrase of mazi dárad.

In this poem even more than in that by Liqá'í, the variable meanings of mazi dárad become apparent – both the double entendre and the mocking tone that Awjí uses when alluding to the ultimate powerlessness of the persecutors to deter the joy he feels in giving his life for a Cause that he knows will endure far beyond these deeds and this point in time. In the end, he looks forward to having his conscious mind view his lifeless body after his execution, because he feels assured that this literal detachment of the soul and its association with the body will be a felicitous sensation.

180 "Speaking flowers" is a Persian idiomatic expression meaning "having a happy conversation."

181 Another Persian idiom meaning "sweet and beautiful smile."

182 A double entendre – the word could mean "agitated" or "enamored."

183 Those with a heavy or difficult soul. The word means "niggardly," implying here one who does not give up his life easily, one who does not die easily or accept things easily. It is a reference to one who is spiritually weak and very much attached to his material life.

184 This poem by Husayn Qaráchidághí is based on a tablet of 'Abdu'l-Bahá which begins with the line: "Lovers, cast away the robe of existence and put on a red robe of the martyr's blood." In this tablet 'Abdu'l-Bahá describes the characteristics of the honored robe of truth which never gets old and never needs repair but day by day becomes more beauteous and splendid. This poem is published in *Andalíb*, vol. 14, no. 55, p. 41.

185 Gnostics.

186 A garment which kings and rulers bestow on someone who is being honored.

187 This poem is from *Payám-i-Bahá'í*, no. 192, November 1995, p. 15. This poem was written by Dr. Sírús Rawshaní before his execution on December 27, 1981. This is a most delightful poem. It contains traditional elements, but not in a traditional fashion. It switches quickly from the imagery of the seeker on the path of the Friend to the specific circumstances of the poet's impending martyrdom. It has a comforting tone because the speaker, well aware of impending doom, speaks light-heartedly about his meager station while acknowledging that this unique opportunity exalts him beyond the kings of the earth.

188 A common image in scripture, usually representing the pure soul or the pure faith of a believer. See the parable of the Pearl of Great Price (Matthew 13:45-46) and the mystical middle English poem "The Pearl."

189 An allusion to Bahá'u'lláh, *The Hidden Words*, #1 from the Persian: "O YE PEOPLE THAT HAVE MINDS TO KNOW AND EARS TO HEAR! The first call of the Beloved is this: O mystic nightingale! Abide not but in the rose-garden of the spirit. O messenger of the Solomon of love! Seek thou no shelter except in the Sheba of the well-beloved, and O immortal phoenix! Dwell not save on the mount of faithfulness. Therein is thy habitation, if on the wings of thy soul thou soarest to the realm of the infinite and seekest to attain thy goal."

190 *Mulk* refers to the earthly dominion and *malakút* to the celestial dominion. The sense is that the speaker's station is the envy of the dwellers of earth and heaven.

191 The poet's name is Sírús (from Cyrus, the great Persian king).

192 This poem is from *Payám-i-Bahá'í*, no. 201, August 1996, p. 43. We have changed the couplets into quatrains because of the clear caesura in most lines. We have also changed the title from the original "Hiking the Skirt."

193 Here the poet may be referring to the four fundamental elements of earth, air, fire, and water (the elements that constitute the world of creation), but he is becoming transformed (as in alchemy) from a baser form of earth and water to a more ephemeral form of fire and air.

194 The "four walls" (*chárdívár*) refers to man's body from which the soul ascends as would a bird from a cage.

195 The hiking up of one's skirt is a Persian idiomatic expression meaning "to disdain" or "to walk away arrogantly."

196 This poem is from 'Abdí, *Gulzár-i-'Ishq*, p. 89.

197 This poem is from Rawhání, *Shahádat va Shahámat*, pp. 43-45. It is modern and terse, not in traditional couplets or images.

198 Published in *Payám-i-Bahá'í*, no. 197, April 1996, p. 13.

199 This poem is from *Shahádat va Shahámat*, p. 37-42. It is written by Sarkish in memory of the martyr 'Atá'u'lláh Yávarí. We have taken liberties with this poem because it is written in a modern style which does not have the natural structure of the couplet form.

200 *Pákbáz*: a word which means those who risk all they have in gambling, those who give away whatever they have.

201 Payám is the martyr's son.

202 The name of the martyr 'Atá'u'lláh.

203 The "city" alludes to the Heavenly Kingdom, the New Jerusalem, or possibly the "City of Certitude" to which Bahá'u'lláh so often alludes in *The Kitáb-i-Iqán*. Here we observe attaining certitude as a conscious effort resulting from the believer's decision to abandon attachment to the concerns of the earthly realm.

204 Mr. Shápúr Markazí was arrested and imprisoned shortly after the Islamic revolution in Iran. This poem was printed in Persian in *'Andalíb*, vol. 5, no. 19, Summer 1986, p. 45. It depicts the deep sorrow and anguish of Shápúr at being separated from his family, particularly from his son and daughter. His despair is temporarily relieved when he learns that they have come to visit him, only to hear from the guard that this is the last visit because he will soon be executed.

However, the poem is much more than a mere recitation of these emotions. After the final visit, we hear another voice, the inner voice of the spirit advising Shápúr to steel himself for the honor and glory of sacrificing himself for his Beloved (Bahá'u'lláh). To do this, Shápúr knows on a rational level that, having said a final farewell to his loved ones, he must now put them out of his mind and leave them to God so that he can focus on the task ahead of him: facing his execution nobly, with detachment, without pleading for mercy and, most importantly, without recanting his faith in Bahá'u'lláh.

Structurally, then, the poem has the same three distinct sections and moods that remind one of the internal dialogue on much the same theme in George Herbert's 17th century poem "The Collar": (a) a sense of anticipation and longing, (b) a sense of utter loss and despair, and (c) a resolve to set aside earthly concerns and focus on the bounty of his station.

205 The image of the firm cord here represents the Covenant and the protection it offers the faithful believer.

206 This poem is from *'Andalíb*, vol. 2, no 5, Winter 1983, p. 58. It reads somewhat like the quality and frequency of the irony we find in the paradoxes in the Petrarchan conceits of the Renaissance (love as a war; the beloved as the cruel enemy; the lover as both the cause of the heart's pain and as the heart's physician). This poem contains a similar kind of juxtaposition of emotions with contrary events. The resulting irony, while not unusual in poetry of this vein, is quite convincing when the words are penned by one whose ultimate fate is to suffer real horror, imprisonment and martyrdom, as opposed to the Petrarchan love whose plaint is largely a literary commonplace.

207 This line alludes to the romantic tradition of the Friend who, like a lover that is arrogant and remote, suddenly relents and returns the lover's affection.

208 Mansúr Halláj was the famous Súfí who was killed while announcing "I am God." Mansúr is thus a symbol for deviation from the conventional ecclesiastical beliefs, a deviation which causes severe persecution. The name also symbolizes the one who has esoteric knowledge and proclaims an idea that is not understood by the ignorant masses.

209 From 'Abdí, *Gulzár-i-'Ishq*, p. 94.

210 The reason for my pride and honor.

211 Qurfah: a high place, the word is used in the Qur'án referring to the paradise: "But those who keep their duty to their Lord, for them are high places, above them higher places, built (for them), wherein river flows. (It is) the promise of Alláh. Alláh fails not in (His) promise." From Muhammad, *The Holy Qur'án*, 39:20. See also 29:58.

212 "Beloved": probably an allusion to the Manifestation of God, the first creation of God, which in Islamic terminology is light. In Sufí terminology, it means the presence and manifestation of God.

213 This poem is from 'Abdí, *Gulzár-i-'Ishq*, pp. 42-43. Muná Mahmúdnizhád. As mentioned in the introduction, Muná Mahmúdnizhád, seventeen years of age, was one of ten Bahá'í women executed in Shíráz on 18 June 1983. The charge against her was teaching Bahá'í classes to children in a private home.

214 An allusion to the Síyáh-Chál, the dungeon in Tihrán where Bahá'u'lláh first began to receive His Revelation.

215 An allusion to Anís, the youth who was martyred with the Báb and who was tied to the Báb in preparation for the firing squad in such a way that his head lay upon the breast of the Báb.

216 This poem is from 'Azíz Hakímíyán, *Zabán-i-Dívárhá: Majmú'iy-i-Ash'ár-i-Kuhnih va Naw, 'Ishqí, Ijtimá'í, Intiqádí, Fukáhí*, p. 146.

217 Farhád, in the famous poetry of Nizámí, was a mountain digger who was in love with Shírín the daughter of the king of Armenia. He was competing with the king of Persia, Khusraw Parvíz, in loving Shírín. Khusraw made him dig Bísutún Mountain. When the false news of the death of Shírín reached Farhád, he rolled down the mountain and died. *(Dihkhudá)* Farhád is therefore a symbol of extreme devotion to one's beloved.

218 Wooden execution post.

219 This poem is from 'Abdí, *Gulzár-i-'Ishq*, p. 90.

220 Name of a fabulous garden built in the city of the tribe of 'Ád. Refer to Muhammad, *The Holy Qur'án*, 89:6-7. "Hast thou not considered how thy Lord dealt with 'Ád, (of) Iram, having lofty buildings, The like of which were not created in the land."

221 From 'Abdí, *Gulzár-i-'Ishq*, pp. 25-26.

222 From 'Abdí, *Gulzár-i-'Ishq*, p. 126.

223 A Persian idiom: one who has a "sea-heart" is one who is courageous. Here it is used as a double entendre.

224 Job, the Biblical figure noted for his patience in the face of being tested by Satan.

225 From 'Abdí, *Gulzár-i-'Ishq*, p. 91

226 Published in the *Payám-i-Bahá'í*, no. 217, December 1997, p. 44.

227 A Persian expression meaning "to remain absolutely quiet."

228 This poem is from *Payám-i-Bahá'í*, no. 223, July 1998, p. 40.

229 The sour orange is a particular variety of orange that is used in marmalades.

230 No doubt a reference to the orange tree that grew in the courtyard garden of the Báb's home in Shíráz.

231 This passage alludes to the fact that many pilgrims took the fruit from the tree then planted the seeds in other cities and countries so that the plant, like the religion itself, has now spread throughout the world.

232 The Báb was kept in seclusion in the Mountains at Mákú, and the Guardian wanted the Shrine lighted brightly in tribute to the darkness the Prophet of God endured for our sake.

233 This poem appeared in 'Andalíb, under the title "Abhá" ("Two Poems from two non-Bahá'í poets received from the Cradle of the Faith."), vol. 11, no. 41-42, Winter and Spring, 1992, p. 72.

234 Published in Payám-i-Bahá'í, no. 216, November 1997.

235 The word "charming" here (shúrangíz) is the same as the concept of the Beloved as the "Charmer," the one who brings about sedition, tumult, and revolt through his beauty.

236 "Half of the world" is a title for Isfahán. The last word of the title (world) rhymes with the name Isfahán.

237 Most probably a reference to the King of Martyrs and the Beloved of Martyrs.

238 "The Exalted Lord," one of the titles of the Báb.

239 This phrase derives from a name of God mentioned in Bahá'u'lláh, The Seven Vallyes and the Four Valleys, translated by Marzieh Gail et al. in consultation with Ali-Kuli Khan (Wilmette, IL, U.S.A.: Bahá'í Publishing Trust, 1991), p. 50.

240 This poem is from Payám-i-Badí', no. 34, vol. 3 (New York, NY: The Local Spiritual Assembly of the Bahá'ís of New york City, October 1985), p. 11.

241 Nishán: "trace" or "portion" or "share," indicating that no one had the privilege of retaining a share of the Beloved's presence.

242 "Flowing cypress," a metaphorical epithet for the Beloved.

243 Bad luck or ill fortune.

وصال یار

دکتر جان هاچر
دکتر امرالله همّت

فهرست

پیشگفتار		هوشمند فتح اعظم	۹
۱- ای خدا جو خدات میخواند		نعیم اصفهانی	۱۶
۲- گر سالکی ای رهرو در عشق مقدم باش		ورقا(شهید)	۱۷
۳- ای تمام انبیاء حیران تو		ورقا(شهید)	۱۹
۴- وضوی عاشق		ورقا(شهید)	۲۱
۵- بلبلی کو آشیان عمری است در گلزار دارد		استاد محمد علی سلمانی	۲۲
۶- مزه دارد		لقائی کاشانی	۲۳
۷- هوالمقصود		روح الله (شهید)	۲۴
۸- اشک کبوتر		عبدی	۲۷
۹- آه آه ای ارض طا ورقا چه شد		نیرو سینا	۲۹
۱۰- یک تن از آنها حسن بدر منیر		نبیل زرندی	۳۰
۱۱- شرح این عاشقان ببرد از یاد		نعیم اصفهانی	۳۱
۱۲- جز در این دین شنیدهئی عاقل		نعیم اصفهانی	۳۲
۱۳- آن شه ظالم قاجار که تدبیر نداشت		عبدی	۳۳
۱۴- بالاتر از حماسه		عبدی	۳۴
۱۵- ایها الناس ما همه بشریم		نعیم اصفهانی	۳۶
۱۶- ملک ایران بکشور امریک		نعیم اصفهانی	۳۷
۱۷- ای مسلمان خانه ما را دگر ویران مکن		نعیم اصفهانی	۳۸
۱۸- گر حاکم دین بست در میکده ها را		عبدی	۳۹
۱۹- ما به سر جز عشق پاک طلعت ابهی نداریم		ولی الله کمال آبادی	۴۰
۲۰- سیمرغ عشق بر دل ما چون قدم نهاد		عبدی	۴۱

۲۱- خمخانه عشق	عبدی	۴۲
۲۲- دیروز، امروز، فردا،		۴۳
۲۳- بنازم ساحت زیبای زندان	محمد رضا حسامی	۴۴
۲۴- همتی مردانه می‌خواهد ز جان خود گسستن	فخرالدین هوشنگ روحانی	۴۵
۲۵- شب شکنان	بهروز بهشتی	۴۶
۲۶- سامانم اینکه بی سر و سامان نمی‌شوم	صالح زاده سمرقندی	۴۷
۲۷- تا از دل و جان بندۀ درگاه بهائیم	عبدی	۴۸
۲۸- جام بلا	فخرالدین هوشنگ روحانی	۴۹
۲۹- جانا برهت باختن جان مزه دارد	اوجی (شهید)	۵۰
۳۰- جامه باقی	حسین قراچه داغی	۵۱
۳۱- تا سر به قدمگاه تو ای دوست گذارم	سیروس روشنی (شهید)	۵۲
۳۲- دامن کشان		۵۳
۳۳- قلب آتشین	عبدی	۵۴
۳۴- نام یک شهید	فخرالدین هوشنگ روحانی	۵۵
۳۵- جان رقص کنان سوی جنان شد شده باشد	منوچهر حجازی	۵۶
۳۶- خوب جاودانه	فخرالدین هوشنگ روحانی	۵۷
۳۷- نمی‌دانم چرا دل بی‌قرار است	شاپور مرکزی (شهید)	۶۰
۳۸- ای خوش آن لحظه که قلبم هدف تیر شود	اوجی (شهید)	۶۲
۳۹- بیاد شید رُخ	عبدی	۶۳
۴۰- شاهد قدسم اگر باز زجا برخیزد	عبدی	۶۵
۴۱- شهید	عزیز حکیمیان	۶۶
۴۲- آزاده	عبدی	۶۷
۴۳- دور از رُخ توگر شب ما را سحری نیست	عبدی	۶۸

۶۹	عبدی	۴۴- ای بسا ذلت که روزی دولت جاوید گشت
۷۰	عبدی	۴۵- چه میخواهد
۷۱	فرهمند مقبلین	۴۶- ای دل افسرده از نو شاد شو
۷۲		۴۷- چیست این فردوس بر کوه خدا
۷۴		۴۸- ابهی
۷۵	اقدس توفیقی	۴۹- سلام ای موطن محبوب عالم
۷۶	هوشمند فتح اعظم	۵۰- وصال یار

پیشگفتار

از صدای سخن عشق ندیدم خوشتر   یادگاری که در این گنبد دوار بماند

کیست در این جهان که از آفتاب عالمتاب عشق پرتوئی نگرفته و رمز محبتی به گوشش نرسیده یا به گوش دیگری نرسانده باشد. محبت مادر به فرزند، عاشق به معشوق، عشق به طبیعت به زیبائی و امثال آن همگان نمودی از جمال عشق است که جلوه‌گر در همهٔ کائنات است و سبب حیات و حرکت جمیع موجودات.

تعریف و تفصیل عشق و محبت در آثار بهائی بسیار است که اگر جمع آید کتابی مطول می‌شود. مثلاً می‌خوانیم که محبت مصدر ایجاد است محبت علت خلقت است «تجلی رحمانی» است «فیض روحانی» است «سبب ظهور حق در عالم امکان» است «رابطه بین حق و خلق در عالم وجدان» است و نیز می‌خوانیم که شاهد محبت و عشق که در سراپردهٔ ذات احدیت پرده‌نشین بود به مشیت الهی از پرده بیرون افتاد و تجلی و ظهورش «مبداء جمیع عشقها و شوقها و سرمایهٔ همهٔ محبتها و شورها شد» به این تقدیر والاترین مظاهر محبت عشق است که دل را به دلدار حقیقی رساند و بین ما و حق که مبداء و منتهای ما است پیوندی ابدی بخشد.

صفحات تاریخ ادیان آکنده از داستانهائی است که از جانبازی و فداکاریهای نفوسی ممتاز و برگزیده حکایت میکند که چون در هر دور چراغ پرفروغ هدایت از آتش محبت الهی درگرفت شمعهای مردهٔ دلها را با شعله ایمان برافروخت و بسوخت و بگداخت تا آنکه از آن سوختن و گداختن انوار عشق جهان را فراگرفت و چشم روزگار در پرتو تمدن جدیدی روشن شد.

۹

در این زمان که انوار محبت خداوند بیهمتا باردیگر در ظهور بهائی بر جهان تابیده و صبح هدایت دمیده، داستان عاشقانی که از جام صبوحی سرمست شده و از هر چه جز معشوق بریده و در راه محبتش از خود گذاشته اند بسیار است کارنامه این دلدادگان پاکباز چنان شورانگیز است که بیان نتوان کرد.

چه زیبا است حکایت آن جان فشانی که در میدان شهادت چون شمشیر جلاد بجای سر به کلاهش میخورد و آنرا برزمین می افکند چنین زمزمه میکند:

خرم آن عاشق سرمست که در پای حبیب   سرو دستار نداند که کدام اندازد

کجا میتوان دید داستان سوخته جانی را که چون او را به میدان فدا می کشاندند دوش و برش را سوراخ سوراخ کرده در هریک شمعی افروخته مینهادند و در کوچه و بازار میگرداندند در چنین حالی آن عاشق دلسوخته به آواز میخواند:

آنکه دائم هوس سوختن ما میکرد   کاش میآمد و از دور تماشا میکرد

کی دیده و خوانده‌ایم که پدری را با پسر دوازده ساله‌اش دستگیر کرده زنجیر میکنند بعد از چند روز پدر را پیش چشم فرزند بنحوی دردناک بقتل میرسانند و به آن نوجوانی که هنوز بوی شیر از دهان چون شکرش میآمد تکلیف میکنند دست از ایمان خویش بردارد تا به سرنوشت پدر دچار نگردد و در جواب آن طفل معصوم یا بهاء الابهی گویان التماس میکند که زودتر او را به پدر برسانند.

شاید بعضی گمان کنند وقایعی که صد سال پیش رخ داده دیگر در این زمان مصداقی نمی یابد اما تاریخ معاصر ما در ایران آن گمان را به یقین تبدیل میکند.

بهائیان در ایران که زادگاه آئین بهائی است هرگز آزاد نبوده و از دست متعصبین ستمکار راحت و آسایش نداشته‌اند در دوره انقلاب اخیر مظالمی که متوجه پیروان حضرت بهاءالله شد نمایش روح‌پرور دیگری از داستان محبت و وفا بر صحنهٔ روزگار آورد که شرح درد و اشتیاق پیشینیان را تازه کرد و شراب کهن عشق را در جامی تازه به دور آورد. چگونه میتوان فراموش کرد که مثلاً ده نفر از دختران شیراز را به جرم دلدادگی به علل واهی محکوم به اعدام کردند مثلاً گفتند که جرمشان اینست که معلم درس اخلاق بودند و کودکان بهائی را به آداب انسانیت تربیت می‌کردند. در روز واقعه این عروسان ملکوت چنان شاد و خندان به میدان فدا می‌شتافتند که سبب حیرت پاسداران و مأموران اجراء حکم شد از یکی از آنان شنیده شد که میگفت چون آنان را در یک اتوبوس میبردند چنان به ذکر و ثنای الهی و تلاوت مناجات و ترنّم نغمه و سرود مشغول بودند که گوئی به مجلس جشن و سرورشان می برند و وقتی چوبهٔ دار حاضر شد و هر ده نفر را در مقابل هم قصد کشتن کردند هر یک بی قراری میکرد که پیش از دیگری کشته شود و چون نوبتشان میرسید هر یک طناب دار را بوسه میداد سپس به گردن لاغر خویش می انداخت تا با آن طناب بالا روند و به ایوان وصال دوست رسند.

یا چگونه می‌توان به کسی آفرین نگفت که چون او را برای تیرباران به میدان شهادت میبردند آرام و خندان به مأموران هشدار داد که این گلوله نیست که به سوی من می آید این منم که به سوی گلوله میروم.

این وقایع حماسه آفرین را همه کسانی که در وقایع بوده یا خود از آن کسان شنیده بودند نقل کرده و همه موجود است و انشاءالله آن نوشته‌های مستند تدوین و منتشر خواهد شد اما آنچه در این دفتر به همت دو بهائی دانشمند، دکتر امرالله همّت، محققی دانشمند از ایران، و دکتر جان هاجر، ادیبی ارجمند و شاعری ماهر از

آمریکا جمع‌آوری و ترجمه شده نمونه‌ای از اشعاری است که یا شهیدان بهائی قبل از شهادت خود سروده و شرح اشتیاق خویش و احتراق از فراق محبوب آفاق را بیان کرده‌اند و یا از کسانی که داستان نثار جان از آن فدائیان راه عشق چنان متأثرشان کرده و طبعشان را بجوش آورده و به سرودن اشعاری واداشته است، یا آنکه بسیاری از آنان شاعر هم بوده‌اند و کتاب حاضر شعر و شهادت از قدم‌های اولیه‌ای است که خوانندگان غیر ایرانی را با احساسات پر رقتی که شهیدان نازنین امر بهائی را به جانبازی تحریک کرده کم و بیش آشنا می‌کند و خود شاید مقدمه آثار دیگری باشد که به یاد آن سوختگان آتش محبت‌الله در آینده به زبانهای مختلف نوشته شود.

هزار افسوس و دریغ که در جهان امروز ما که از لحاظ معنوی فقر شدیدی عارضش گشته است احساسات لطیف انسان که منبعث از روح الهی اوست نزد اکثری پوشیده مانده از حقیقت خویش منحرف گشته است حتی در این زمینه الفاظ و کلمات نیز معانی واقعی خود را از دست داده‌اند. مثلاً کلمه والای عشق که دُرّ شاهوار خزانه عرفان و ادب ایران است این روزها به نوعی مبتذل چنان به کار میرود که سبب آزردگی خاطر است. کلمه عشق را ملاحظه کنید غالباً در ادبیات و شعر و موسیقی‌های مجری معنائی امروز جز هوسرانی و اطفاء شهوات حیوانی ندارد غافل از اینکه عشق‌بازی دگر و نفس‌پرستی دگر است. یا لفظ شهادت را در اجتماع کنونی برای کسانی به کار می‌برند که با تلقیناتی که به نام دین به آنان شده‌است جان خود را بر سر کارهای غیرانسانی و کشتار بی‌گناهان به نام دین و سیاست از دست می‌دهند به وعدهٔ بهشتی که جمیع لذائذ و تمتّعات را تا ابد برایشان فراهم می‌آورد و عدهٔ دیگری را به هلاکت میرسانند. اما در عرف بهائی شهادت چنین نیست زیرا آنچه حضرت بهاءالله از پیروانش خواسته عشق و محبت است. بهائیان به امید بهشت و ترس از جهنم بعملی دست نمیزنند. حتی فلسفه اطاعت از

احکام دیانت نیز عشق است نه خوف و رجا، میفرمایند تعالیم و احکام را بخاطر محبت به من به کار بندید نه به امید بهشت. حضرت عبدالبهاء در لوحی میفرمایند:

شرط محبت آن است که انسان جان فدای جانان نماید و سرگشته و سودائی گردد و رسوای عالمیان شود

اما مقصود از فدا در امر بهائی آن نیست که انسان برای کسب ثوابی خود را به کشتن دهد، یعنی کشته شدن فی نفسه ثواب و فضیلتی نیست. در این بیان حضرت عبدالبهاء ملاحظه فرمائید:

وقت آن است که جام لبریز گردید و مانند نسیم جانپرور جنت ابهی در آن کشور مشکبیز شوید، از شئون عالم هستی بیزار شوید و در هر رتبه آرزوی نیستی نمائید، شعاع چون بآفتاب رسد محو و نابود گردد و قطره چون به دریا رسد ناپدید شود، عاشق صادق چون به معشوق رسد معدوم شود، انسان تا به مقام فدا قدم ننهد از هر موهبتی محروم گردد، و مقام فدا مقام فنا و نیستی است تا هستی الهی جلوه نماید، و مشهد فدا میدان انقطاعست تا آیات بقا ترتیل گردد، تا توانید از خود بکلی بیزار شوید و گرفتار آن روی پرانوار و چون به این مقام سجود فائز شوید من فی الوجود را در ظل خویش یابید، اینست موهبت کبری اینست سلطنت عظمی اینست حیات بی منتهی، ما دون آن عاقبت خسران

هیچ بهائی نباید در پی آن باشد که خود را به این امید که به مقام شهادت برسد و ثوابی ببرد به خطر اندازد یا به کشتن دهد. بلکه در آثار بهائی میخوانیم که شهادت مقبول است اگر خود واقع گردد یعنی اگر کسی جز جمال دوست نبیند و جز در سبیل عشق و انقطاع و وفا نپوید در آن شاهراه اگر موجباتی پیش آید که ناچار جانش باید نثار جانان گردد البته این فدا مقبول درگاه کبریا است. حضرت بهاءالله مکرر در جواب تقاضای عاشقان جمال مبارکش که آرزوی شهادت کرده‌اند نصیحت فرموده که در عوض وصول به مقام شهادت برخدمت امرالهی قیام کنند و در راه تحقق وحدت عالم انسانی که اراده الهی در این زمان است بکوشند و شهید زنده باشند. حضرت عبدالبهاء در جواب عاشق صادقی که پیراهن تن را تنگ می‌بیند و آرزوی شهادت می‌کند چنین میفرماید:

مقام فدا بسیار مقبول و مطلوب ولی الیوم باید چنان بود که در هر ساعتی شهید گشت و در هر دقیقه هزار جان فدا نمود. اما شهادت یکدفعه جان باختن و تا فضای اوج اعظم تاختن است ولی خوشتر آنکه در این بساط بکمال فرح و انبساط هر آن صد هزار جان فدا نمود و به خدمت امر حضرت احدیت قیام کرد و به میدان بسالت و هدایت بتاخت و جنود ضلالت و ظلمت را به انوار مشرق احدیت متشتت کرد و صفوف سپاه غفلت را در هم شکست و صف جنگ روحانی بیاراست و سپاه معانی ترتیب داد و علم دانائی برافروخت و هجوم شدید بر لشگر جهل و نادانی نمود

پس شهیدانی که در این عصر در ایران با کمال سرور و شجاعت و سرافرازی طناب

دار را بوسه دادند و به استقبال گلوله شتافتند برای آن نبود که برای خود حماسه بیافرینند و طالب نام و نشانی گردند بلکه محو خداوند مهربان بودند که محبوب جهان است و یقین داشتند راهی که میروند آن طریق عشق است خونریزی است ولی شورانگیز است و مطمئن بودند که با فدای جان اثبات محبت بعالم انسانی مینمایند و گوش به پیغام سروش داده میدانستند که عشق و محبت روح حیات در جسم این عالم فانی است محبت سبب تمدن امم در این حیات بی ثبات ما است سبب ترقی جمیع بشر است. اینست که با کمال انقطاع که از خصائص ایمان است آن نفوس دلباخته از افق فدا در نهایت انقطاع درخشیدند و اگر هم دست ظالمان به خونشان رنگین نمی‌شد چه بسا چند صباحی که در این عالم فانی زندگانی می‌نمودند باز عمرشان در خدمت امرالله صرف می‌شد زیرا چون آن سوختگان آتش محبت‌الله اساس و بنیاد هستی را بر عشق نهاده بودند کمال واقعی را نیز در عشق جستند و یافتند و به ملکوت بقا شتافتند.

ما ایرانیان که شاهد فداکاری عزیزانمان بوده و هستیم باید بسیار از همّت جناب همّت و جناب هاچر شکرگذار باشیم که با ترجمه و طبع اشعار مربوط به سرّ فدا قلوب ما را به یاد عاکفان کوی بقا به اهتزاز آوردند و مخصوصاً برای غیر ایرانیان فضای ناآشنائی را گشودند که امید است باعث سرور و امتنانشان باشد.

هوشمند فتح اعظم
سپتامبر ۲۰۰۳

۱

نعیم اصفهانی

ای خدا جو خدات میخواند	حضرت کبریات میخواند
ذات باقی ز عالم فانی	سوی ملک بقات میخواند
ای تو مشتاق و منتظر بشتاب	حق ببزم لقات میخواند
ای زمینی تو آسمانی شو	کز زمین بر سمات میخواند
حق یکتا میان جنگ و جدال	سوی صلح و صفات میخواند
بندگانش غریق بحر هلاک	از برای فدات میخواند
شاه دین ای گدای راه نشین	در صف انبیات میخواند
جانب صلح کل صلاح عموم	سوی دین بهات میخواند
سعی در اتحاد من فی الارض	هست بر ذمهٔ خلایق فرض

۲

ورقا (شهید)

هوالله

گر سالکی ای رهرو در عشق مقدم باش	بر نفس مسلط شو در عقل مسلم باش
ای جوهر نورانی و ای فطرت انسانی	از عالم حیوانی دم درکش و آدم باش
تو ذات من و مائی او وصافی و اسمائی	خورشیدی و دریائی رخشندهٔ و ملطم باش
هشدار که مست استی غافل ز الست استی	گر دوست پرست استی محرم شو و محرم باش
از فیض خدا مهراس خود را بخدا بشناس	ای روح خدا در ناس چون عیسی مریم باش
گر ز اهل دلی یا هو صاحب نفسی میجو	با آنکه صدیق است او همره شو و همدم باش
هین فرّهٔ شاهی بین اسرار الهی بین	روح متباهی بین چون نور مجسم باش
با اهل صفا بنشین انوار حقیقت بین	اندر ره علم و دین ثابت شو و محکم باش
با عشق و محبت شو از اهل مودّت شو	رو داخل جنت شو خارج ز جهنم باش
در مشرق استفتاح درکش قدح ارواح	در لیل ظلم مصباح در ارض کرم یم باش
این گوهره چون سفتم در سر و خفا گفتم	آن دمدمه بنهفتم هان عارف آندم باش
اول شو و آخر شو باطن شو و ظاهر شو	کاشف شو و ساتر شو فاتح شو و خاتم باش
جام احدیّت نوش ثوب ابدیّت پوش	در علم هویّت کوش عالم شو و اعلم باش
آن ساکت صائح بین آن لطف نصائح بین	آن کوبهٔ لائح بین آسوده و بیغم باش
در کسوت عریانی سرّیست به پنهانی	ما را تو چه میدانی مخدوم مکرّم باش
گر جرعهٔ حقّ نوشی چشم از همه در پوشی	ای ذرّه چه میجوشی ایقطره بیایم باش
از خلق مجو پیشی کت نوش شود نیشی	تا کی طلبی بیشی بسیار ولی کم باش
مقصود ترا گوید بشتاب که میگوید	بشنو که چه میگوید برخیز و مصمّم باش

۱۷

وصال یار

در نـور تجّلایــش شــو محــو تماشــایش در طـرهٔ سـودایش آشـفته و درهـم بـاش
شــو داخــل ایــن بــستان در زمـرهٔ سرمـستان ایـن جـام زمـا بـستان و آنگـاه بـرجم بـاش
آن صبح دمید از شـام روشـن شـد از او ایّـام ای اختـر مـا بـر بـام رو نیّـر اعظـم بـاش
زیـن مرحلــه بیــرون شــو از طیــر وفـا بــشنو گر سالکی ای رهرو در عـشق مقدّم بـاش

۱۸

۳

ورقا (شهید)

ای تمــام انبیــاء حیــران تــو	اولیــا مبهــوت و سرگردان تــو
صد هـزاران نفـس قـدس و روح پـاک	جـان پـاک افکنـده در راهـت بخـاک
صد هـزاران آدم انـدر کـوی تـو	ربّنــا انّــا ظلمنــا گـوی تــو
صد هـزاران غرقـه چـون نـوح نجی	گشته در طوفـان بجـودت ملتجـی
صد هـزاران چـون خلیـل سـوخته	رفتـه انــدر آتــش افروختــه
تـا شـده در بوتـهٔ حـبّ بـی غـشا	گلســتان گردیــده بــر روی آتـشا
صد هـزاران همچـو اسماعیـل راد	کـرده قربــان تـو خـود را از وداد
صد هـزاران چـون کلیـم از نــور تـو	اوفتــاده منصعـق بــر طـور تـو
صد هـزاران همچـو ایّـوب صبـور	در بــلای تـو شــده عبـد شکـور
صد هـزاران همچـو عیسـی در جهان	بـر سـر دار ولایــت داده جــان
صد هـزاران بنــده در منهــاج تـو	چـون محمّـد عـارج معـراج تـو
صد هـزاران اولیــاء، ارواح پـاک	در ره تـو ریختـه خونشـان بخـاک
صد هـزاران کشـتگانت در ولا	چــون حسیـن انــدر زمیـن کـربلا
در زمینهـا ذرّه‌ای از خـاک نیسـت	کــان مطّهــر از دمــاء پـاک نیست
ای بســا ابحــار و انهــار و عیـون	گشته جـاری در فراقـت از عیـون
هــر کجــا هســت آتشـی افروختـه	یـا کـه برقـی خرمنـی را سـوخته
شعله‌ای از راه قلــب مقبلــی است	یا شـرار سینـهٔ صاحب دلیسـت
راه مشتاقانـت ای ابهـی صفـات	در تهیّـج ایـن ریـاح عاصفـات
تابش خورشیـد از تیـزی تـو اسـت	حمـرت عـالم ز خـون ریـزی تواست
ز آتـش عشـق تـو ای سلطان جـان	سـوخته جــان و روان انـس و جـان

سینه‌ای نبود که بریان تو نیست   دیده‌ای نبود که گریان تو نیست
هرکجا باشد دلی پر خون ز تواست   هست هرجا خاطری محزون ز تواست

٤

ورقا (شهید)

وضوی عاشق

مرا کشتن روا باشد ز دست چون توئی قاتل	اگر کشتن خطا باشد بشر را عالم و عاقل
مرا در لجّهٔ عشقت نباشد شوق بر ساحل	اگرچه نیست در عالم کسی بر غرق خود شایق
خدا را بس کن ای ناصح ازین گفتار بیحاصل	نبیند ناصحان چشمم نگردد دیگر از رویش
که نبود جز بخون دل وضوی عاشقان کامل	گمان بردی نمازم را وضو نبود ندانستی
ندانم فاضلت خوانم و یا خودگویمت عادل	بشارت دادی از ابرو فکندی در خم گیسو
بدین اخلاق روحانی امید عالم عامل	بدین خویی و رعنائی هلاک عاشق عارف
که ذوق عشق جانان را چه داند زاهد جاهل	اگر بتوانی ای شیدا مکن اسرار دل پیدا
از آن ساعت که جا دادم غم عشق ترا در دل	دگر غمهای گیتی را نمانده هیچ تأثیری
اگرچه این متاع کم نباشد مر تو را قابل	نثار مقدمت چیزی ندارم غیر جان لایق
دلا گر زندگی خواهی مباش ازین سخن غافل	بجز وصلش حبیبا نرا نباشد مایهٔ هستی
که گر گوید بلب یکدم بسوزد جسم آب و گل	نواها هست ورقا را ز عشقت در دل شیدا

۵

استاد محمد علی سلمانی

بلبلی کو آشیان عمری است در گلزار دارد   کی نظر از گل بپوشد، کی خبر از خار دارد

گاه گرید، گاه خندد، گاه سازد، گاه زارد   گاه حیران و غزلخوان دیده بر دلدار دارد

غرقه در دریای عشقش کی نظر دارد به ساحل   او به جان مشتاق موج است و ز ساحل عار دارد

بر سر بازار عشقش جان فروشان راست راهی   خود پسند بی ادب کی ره در این بازار دارد

آنکه محو آفتاب است کی نظر دارد به ظلمت   آنکه عشق یار دارد کی خبر ز اغیار دارد

هر که در راه تو پوید دست و دل از جان بشوید   جز رضای تو نجوید هر که با تو کار دارد

وه عجب آب و هوائی دارد این باغ الهی   خاکش از آتش، گل آتش، ابر آتش بار دارد

خامۀ عبدالبهاء یا خضر، بازآمد ز ظلمت   یا چو مرغی آب حیوان جاری از منقار دارد

هر دلی عشق بهاء دارد ندارد حب دنیا   باز سلطان کی نظر بر لاشۀ مردار دارد

۶

لقائی کاشانی

مزه دارد

بـر روی مهـت زلـف پریـشان مـزه دارد   پیــرامُن گــل ســنبل بیجــان مــزه دارد
جـان آمـده برلـب چـه شـود یـار درآیـد   جـان بـر لـب و لـب بـر لـب جانـان مزه دارد
هی هی چه خیال و چه تمنای محال است   درویــش و پـــذیرائی ســلطان مـــزه دارد
نبـود غمــم ازکـشته شـدن بـر سـر کـویش   قربــانی ایــن طـایر بــی جـان مــزه دارد
ضوضای عوام از پی و طبل و دهل از پیش   مــن رقـص کنـان جانـب میـدان مزه دارد
ای شـیخ زمـن بگـذر و مـنعم مکـن از عـشق   کـاین دل شـده را طعـن رقیبـان مـزه دارد
بیهوده مکش رنج ومکن وعظ و مده پند   در جـان مـن ایـن آتـش سـوزان مزه دارد
مــا غرقــه دریــای فنــائیم لقـائی   بـا مـا سخن از شـدت بـاران مزه دارد

٧

روح الله (شهید)

هوالمقصود

جام می را ساقیا سرشار کن	طور دل را از میّت پرنار کن
ساغری در ده ز صهبای الست	تا بهوش آیم من مخمور مست
بردرم استار وهم و هم گمان	بر پرم بر اوج هفتم آسمان
بگذرم زین تیره دام آب و خاک	ره سپر گردم بروحستان پاک
وارهم زین ملک پر رنج و محن	رو نمایم سوی روحانی وطن
بشنوم از گلشن جان بوی دوست	بازگردم چون نسیم از کوی دوست
بامعطّر نفحه های جانفزا	با مبارک مژده های غمزدا
بر ملا گویم به احباب دیار	یوم میثاق است یاران البدار
البدار ای عاشقان روی دوست	رو کنید از جان به سوی کوی دوست
ای رفیقان دم غنیمت بشمرید	امر حق را نصرت و یاری کنید
همّتی یاران که این امر مبین	منتشر گردد در اقطار زمین
کوششی یاران که گردد منتشر	در جهان آیات ربّ مقتدر
تا بهوش آیند این مخلوق مست	از ظنون و وهم بردارند دست
چشمشان از نور حقّ روشن شود	خارزار قلبشان گلشن شود
همّت ای یاران که وقت خدمت است	گاه کسب فیض و یوم نصرتست
رو نمائید ای احبّای بها	سوی عالم با علمهای هدی
این چنین فرمود سلطان قدم	در کتاب اقدس خود بر امم
هر که بنماید به امر حقّ قیام	می نماید نصرتش ربّ الانام

وصال یار

هرکه جان در عهد حق سازد فدا / سوی او ناظر بود وجه خدا
ساقیا جامی کرم کن از عطا / تا شوم طاهر ز هر جرم و خطا
گرچه عصیانم فزون‌ست از شمار / لیک از فضل حقّم امیدوار
مرحبا ای ساقی بزم قدم / رشحه‌ای افشان بر این خاک از کرم
تا ز جودت ذرّه‌ها تابان شود / نزد جانان قابل قربان شود
کی شود یا رب که اندر کوی تو / جان فدا سازم به عشق روی تو
خرّم آنروزی که در میدان عشق / جان دهم اندر ره جانان عشق
ای خوش آن حینی که گویم آشکار / وصف سلطان بها بر روی دار
ای خدا آنروز کی خواهد شدن / که شوم فارغ ازین پژمرده تن
رو نمایم سوی فردوس بقا / سبز و خرّم گردم از فیض لقا
اندر این بیدای حرمان سوختم / و از شرار نار هجر افروختم
برقع از رخ بر فکن ای شاه جان / تا شود روشن ز نورت آسمان
ای شه میثاق ای سلطان عهد / ای زنارت مشتعل فاران عهد
ای که خود را خوانده‌ای عبدالبهاء / مرتفع ز امر تو رایات هدی
مطلّع ز اسرار سبحانی توئی / منبع آثار یزدانی توئی
چون الف قائم به امر کردگار / هستی ای شاهنشه ذوالاقتدار
لیک خاضع در عبودیت چو با / نزد باب روضهٔ ربّ البهاء
ای تو سدرهٔ امر را غصن عظیم / وی تو فرع منشعب ز اصل قدیم
ای که هستی مشرق وحی خدا / از تو روشن دیدهٔ اهل بهاء
نظره‌ای از لطف بر این طیر زار / که از هجرت گشته بی صبر و قرار
ز آتش بُعد تو سوزان دل شدم / زد شرر هجر تو بر آب و گلم

الغیاث ای شهریار ملک دل 	 از فراقت گشته قلبم مشتعل
سوختم شاها من از نار فراق 	 اندرین بیدای هجر و اشتیاق
کن خلاص این طیر را از دام غم 	 ای ملیک فضل و سلطان کرم
"درلیاقت منگر و در قدرها 	 بنگر اندر فضل خود ای ذوالعطا"

وصال یار

۸

عبدی

اشک کبوتر

صبحگاهان که صبا بوسه به گلها میزد
دو کبوتر که یکی داشت به لب غنچهٔ عشق
شب پره از لب نوشین شقایق مدهوش
ژاله خندید و گل و سبزه به وجد آمد از آن
گاه در حجله‌ای از نسترن و یاس سپید
گاه در برکه ای از آب و گهی بال زنان
در همان لحظه که آهسته سخن میگفتند
ناگهان بوی گل مریم و نسرین به مشام
تا یکی جست بر آن مرقد گلپوش و سرود
گفت معشوقه که آهسته‌تر ای مایهٔ عمر
هر کجا سوسن و گل بود نه جای طربست
لاله از خون شهیدان شده گلگون و از آن
گشت شرمنده سبکبال از آن گفته خویش
خیمه زد در همه جا سایه خورشید و هنوز
سالها پیش پس از مرگ شه دیو سرشت
خصم ناپاک در آن مهلکه با توسن خشم
دور از همهمه و فتنه زاغان پلید
لیک ز آنجا که شود آنچه خدا خواسته است

سایه بال و پری خلوت گلزار شکست
از پی آن دگری پرزد و بر شاخه نشست
آن دو سرمست و سبکبال در آغوش بهار
صحن گلزار شده خرّم از این بوس و کنار
سینه از شبنم گلبرگ سحر می‌شستند
دانه از خرمن گلگشت چمن می جستند
تا که از حیله صیّاد نیفتند به دام
میرسید از گذر خاک مزاری آرام
نازپرورد من، اینجا همه عشق است و امید
بعد از آن قطره اشکیش ز رخسار چکید
باشد این خرمن گل، گورشهیدی ناکام
در شفق دیده گریان فلک شد گلفام
اشک معشوقه به دل آتشی افروخته بود
گفتگو بر سر آن عاشق دلسوخته بود
دسته دوزخیان کرد عیان چهره زشت
رفت خاموش کند اختر ورقای بهشت
پدری با پسرش بسته به زنجیر جفا
به رضایش که همه خیر بود داده رضا

۲۷

وصال یار

هان دگر این چه هیاهوست پدر می‌شنوی / آسمان بهر شما عاقبت امروز طپید
داد پاسخ پدر اینگونه به دُردانه خویش / الوداع ای پسرم لحظه موعود رسید
درب پُوسیده زندان بلا قهقهه زد / آمد ابلیس که وقت سخن و نجوا نیست
گفت با قامت افروخته آن کودک عشق / بچه شیر در این کنج قفس چون ما نیست
لحن جلاد شد آرام که ای سروروان / هیچکس غنچه شاداب تو پر پر نکند
گفت آن کیست ز عشاق جمال قدمش / که ز خاک قدمش غالیه بر سر نکند
خنجر حاجب سفّاک چو برقی ز سحاب / بر زمین آمد و پهلوی پدر را بدرید
چونکه فرزند نصیحت نشنید از جلاد / فلکی گردن او بسته و در بند کشید
سوخت پروانه و با شمع وجودش می‌گفت / آه آسوده شدی جانم از این رنج و بلا
هرگز از بخت جوان خاطر ما شاد نگشت / ما که رفتیم و چنین بود به سر قسمت ما
محشر روز خدا گشت در آن روز عیان / خون پاک شهدا ریخت به اوراق زمان
آنهمه ظلم که ز آن مردم درّنده بدید / مانده جلاد و سرانگشت تحیّر به دهان
شیون و زاری اطفال به افلاک رسید / مادران در پی فرزند به میدان فدا
مادر شیردلان گفت به آوای بلند / جان این کودک دلبند به قربان بها
شرح جانبازی ورقا که بدینجا برسید / دسته‌ای مرغ هوا بال زنان می‌رفتند
هر دوچون اوج گرفتند به گردون سپهر / شرح این قصّه به مرغان دگر می‌گفتند
میکشد شعله دلم از قفس سینه تنگ / آتشی کز تف آن پرتو خورشید دمید
روید از قطره اشکی که بر این خاک چکید / لاله سُرخ، ز آرمگه ورقای شهید

۹

نیروسینا

آه آه ای ارض طا ورقا چه شد	مرغ باغ طلعت ابهی چه شد
آن تذرو گلشن توحید کو	و آن غزال قدس این صحرا چه شد
ای صبا فرزند دلبندش کجاست	آن خوش الحان بلبل گویا چه شد
آن نهال نورس نوخیز کو	و آن گل نشکفتهٔ رعنا چه شد
قمری موزون خوش آهنگ کو	طوطی شیرین شکرخا چه شد
جوجهٔ سیمرغ قاف قرب کو	بچهٔ آهوی برّها چه شد
صوت روح افزای روح‌الله کو	نغمهٔ جانپرور ورقا چه شد
بی حضورش انجمن را نور نیست	ای دریغ آن انجمن آرا چه شد
قتل او را حاجب ار واجب شمرد	آن مسجّل قتل و آن فتوی چه شد
کس نداند جسم زارش در کجاست	و آن منور هیکل روحا چه شد
گر در آتش رفت ابراهیم‌وار	آن گل و آن لالهٔ حمرا چه شد
ور چو یونس در دهان حوت رفت	آن خروج بعدش از دریا چه شد
ور چو یوسف گرگش از هم بردرید	آن قمیص کذب خون پالا چه شد
ورنه گرگش خورد و در چاه اوفتاد	شرح دلو و قال یا بشری چه شد
ور چو یحیی خون او در طشت ریخت	آن سر و آن پیکر زیبا چه شد
ور چو عیسی بر فراز دار رفت	آن هجوم قوم و آن غوغا چه شد
گرسرش از تن جدا شد چون حسین	آن تن پاکیزهٔ نورا چه شد
ورشد از شمشیر و خنجر ریز ریز	کس نمی‌گوید که آن اعضا چه شد
نیّرو سینا چو نی نالند زار	کان رفیق با وفای ما چه شد

۱۰

نبیل زرندی

یک تن از آنها حسن بدر منیر	در وفا گردیده موی او چو شیر
زاهد و دارای علم و با عمل	با تحمل در بلایا چون حمل
در شب آخر چو رخشان آفتاب	آمده محبوب ابهایش بخواب
گفته او را کای حسن شد بی الم	اسم تو در لوح سربازان رقم
کر تو را نبود باین معنی رضا	گوی بر من تا بگردانم قضا
گفته لا والله خواهم صدروان	تا ببازم در قدومت رایگان
شاه گفتش چون رضائی ای صدیق	این دو تن هم بایدت بودن رفیق
چونکه شد بیدار از آن رؤیا حسن	با رفیقان گفت خواب خویشتن
هر دو گفتندش که اوهامست این	می‌شویم آزاد ما فردا یقین
گفت نی نی یا رضا یا نارضا	می‌شویم امروز ما هر سه فدا
قول محبوبست و دروی نی خلاف	با رضای او نمائید اعتراف
ساعتی نگذشت کز انجایگاه	هر سه را بردند سوی قتلگاه
هر سه تن دادند جان اما حسن	با سرور و آن دو با آه و حزن

۱۱

نعیم اصفهانی

شرح این عاشقان ببرد از یاد	ذکر مجنون و قصهٔ فرهاد
جانب مقتل آنچنان رفتند	که بحجله نمی‌رود داماد
حسن او کرد خواجگان بنده	بندگان را ز بند خویش آزاد
آن یکی در غم و شکنجه بماند	آن دگر در بلا و رنج افتاد
آن یکی خانمان بر آتش زد	و آن دگر خانواده داد بباد
آن یکی مال و آن دگر فرزند	آن یکی جاه و آن دگر جان داد
با هزاران مخرّب این بانی	کرد این خانه را چسان آباد
اندرین موج فتنه و طوفان	پایهٔ دین ببین چگونه نهاد
حیّر العقل جلّ سلطانه	و علاقد ره و برهانه

۱۲

نعیم اصفهانی

جز در این دین شنیده‌ئی عاقل	بتمنای موت مستعجل
جز بدارالسلام کس دیدی	کرده خود را بدست خود بسمل
جز بطهران شنیده‌ئی که سه ماه	نامهٔ قتل خود برد عاقل
جز بزنجان شنیده‌ئی مادر	که بقتل پسر شود عاجل
جز بشیراز کس بشوق دهد	مژدگانی بقاتل جاهل
هیچ کس جز در اصفهان داده است	دیت قتل خود بمستقبل
هیچ دیدی بجز بعشق آباد	کس شفاعت نماید از قاتل
هیچ کس گشته است جز در یزد	وقت کشتن باین سخن قائل
لم ارد ناصراً لینصرنی	بل ارد ناظراً لینظرنی

۱۳

عبدی

آن شه ظالم قاجار که تدبیر نداشت	خبر از عاقبت بازی تقدیر نداشت
در صف حاکم دین از پی خشنودی شاه	گشت محکوم، هر آن بنده که تقصیر نداشت
بست محبوب جهان را به چنان سلسله‌ای	که فلک طاقت آن حلقهٔ زنجیر نداشت
آگه از سر پریشانی عشاق نشد	آنکه دل در خم آن زلف گره‌گیر نداشت
نازم اقبال شهیدی که به فرمان قضا	سر نهاد و غمی از سطوت شمشیر نداشت
شیخ مسکین که ندارد خبر از دانش و دین	کاشکی آنهمه خود خواهی و تزویر نداشت
عبدیا دیدهٔ این خلق اگر کور نبود	واحدالعین، به کف حربهٔ تکفیر نداشت
گر عبث بود تجلی بشارات بهاء	این چنین پرتو انوار جهانگیر نداشت

۱۴

عبدی

بالاتر از حماسه

ای طیر سینه سرخ و همای شهید عشق   گر ریخت خون پاک تو از ظلم شیعیان
امّا نرفته از دل و هرگز نمی‌رود   بانگ بشارتی که رساندی به گوش جان
ای روح سربلند که بعد از شهادتت   پنجاه سال عرش تو آرامشی نداشت
نازم ترا که در کف دشمن ز عشق دوست   غیر از نثار گوهر جان خواهشی نداشت
در حیرتم که خصم زبون، بهر قتل تو   کردی بسیج از چه قشون و سپاه را
روزی که ریخت باد قضا بر سر نفوس   بعد از وقوع حادثه، خاک سیاه را
شلیک بر کبوتر بام حرم نمود   تیری که قلب نقطهٔ اولی هدف گرفت
آن سینه‌ای که قبلهٔ راز انیس بود   تیر از جفای خلق زمان، صف به صف گرفت
باری گلوله، بار نخستین که شرم داشت   از آنکه قصد سینهٔ عرش خدا کند
لیکن نمود شرحه، به تقدیر ثانوی   تا شاید آنکه خلق زمانه حیا کند
امّا حیا نکرد و پس از قرن دیگری   یورش به خاک کوی تو بهر ثواب کرد
غافل که با کلنگ جهالت به دست خویش   بنیان ملک و خانهٔ خود را خراب کرد
سرکوب شد به موجب فرمان شیخ و شاه   هر جا ز معجزات تو چون ازدحام شد
شبدیز عشق بود و سمند غرور عقل   آن اسب سرکشی که به پیش تو رام شد
نشناخت خلق شیعه، تراگر چه آمدی   همراه معجزات و علامات ظاهره
لیکن بس است معجز حق را در این زمان   عشق انیس و حجت و قدّوس و طاهره
کتمان کنند و ذمّ تو از ترس یکدیگر   قومی که پای منبر و محراب و کرسی‌اند
امّا منادیان تو آزاده و شجاع   چون شهپران قلعهٔ شیخ طبرسی‌اند

برگو به رغم مفتی بی دین چه کرده‌ای   کاینسان هنوز چون پدرش با تو دشمن است
یا بر علیه حکم شریعت چه گفته‌ای   کان را جزای محکمه، زندان و کشتن است
اکنون بجای ظلمت ما کو چراغ شب   روشن ز نور گنبد و صحن مقام تست
آنجا که آفتاب طلایی، سحرگهان   قندیل این سپهر درخشان ز بام تست
گفتم حماسه‌ای بسرایم ز آب چشم   تا در زمین، ستارهٔ تابان شود همی
لیکن تو در زمین و به طومار آسمان   بالاتر از حماسه، به تاریخ عالمی

۱۵

نعیم اصفهانی

ایها الناس ما همه بشریم	بندۀ یک خدای دادگریم
خواهران و برادران همیم	چون زیک مادر و زیک پدریم
هم بیک صورت و بیک هیئت	هم زیک عنصر و زیک گهریم
متشکل باحسن التقویم	متصور باعدل الصوریم
هیچ درّنده جنس خود ندرد	ما چرا نوع خویشتن بدریم
مدّتی رنج دشمنی بردند	حالیا عیش دوستی ببریم
متوطن درون خانۀ تنگ	از چه رو دشمنان یکدگریم
همه دانیم باریک داریم	گرفریب ستم گران نخوریم
میزند صاحب جهان فریاد	بستگان رسته بندگان آزاد

۱۶

نعیم اصفهانی

ملک ایران بکشور امریک	می‌فرستد بمیمنت تبریک
که مبارک قدوم مرکز عهد	باد میمون بخطهٔ امریک
شمس مشرق برآمد از مغرب	لیک مشرق از آن نشد تاریک
کآیت وحدت حقیقی حق	که ندارد بدیل و شبه و شریک
کرده یک خطه مشرق و مغرب	کرده یک فرقه دیلم و تا جیک
داده دلها چنان بهم پیوند	که نیابند تا ابد تفکیک
گرچه از راه آب و گل دورند	لیک از راه جان و دل نزدیک
گفت و البته ساری و جاری است	در ممالیک و ملک حکم ملیک
که بود موعد و داد بشر	آمده وقت اتحاد بشر

۱۷

نعیم اصفهانی

ای مسلمان خانه ما را دگر ویران مکن — خانه‌ات آباد ما را بی سر و سامان مکن
در فراق مادران ای حاکم شرع مبین — چشم اطفال بهائی را چنین گریان مکن
فتح و پیروزی ترا خوش باد اما بیش از این — مردم بی خانمان را زار و سرگردان مکن
ای مسلمان گرستم بر خلق دنیا می‌کنی — نسبت خود با علی شاه جوانمردان مکن
قتل و غارت نیست در قانون دین مصطفی — گر بدین بی اعتقادی تکیه بر قرآن مکن
لحظه‌ای اندیشه کن ای شیخ در فتوای خویش — شرع را تسلیم فکر مردم نادان مکن
آتش مهرو ستم را بیش از این دامن مزن — قلب مخلوق خدا را عاری از وجدان مکن
گفت عبدی با دلی خونین و آهی آتشین — ای مسلمان خانهٔ ما را دگر ویران مکن

۱۸

عبدی

گر حاکم دین بست در میکده‌ها را	بگشاد در کوچهٔ تزویر و ریا را
ای وای که این قوم ستم پیشه دریدند	مانند سلف پردهٔ آزرم و حیا را
فریاد از این قوم ستمکاره که کشتند	مظلومترین بنده و مخلوق خدا را
از آه شهیدان بها سوزد و نالد	این سینه که دارد هوس تیر بلا را
ای شیخ بزن تا بتوانی پی تکفیر	با تیر ستم قافلهٔ اهل بها را
غافل مشو اما که اگر هست خدائی	هنگام دُعا می‌شنود نالهٔ ما را
گر حکم وفا نیست به قاموس مسائل	در بارهٔ هر مسئله حدّی است جفا را
عبدی نکند ظلم و شود عارف حق بین	بشناسد اگر شیخ ستم پیشه خدا را

۱۹

ولی الله کمال آبادی

با جهان و خواستارانش سر و سودا نداریم	ما به سر جز عشق پاک طلعت ابهی نداریم
بغض و کین با هیچ کائن، حبّ این دنیا نداریم	در دل ما نیست جائی جز برای عشق دلبر
ما به جان مشتاق دردیم، از بلا پروا نداریم	بهر درد عشق جانان هیچ داروئی نجوئیم
آبمان از سرگذشته، بیمی از دریا نداریم	بی سبب ما را ز موج و خشم طوفانها مترسان
ما جهان خواهیم و این را از کسی حاشا نداریم	تهمت جاسوسی و بیگانگی ما را نزیبد
در جهان جنگ و جدل با هیچکس اصلاً نداریم	ما برادر یار و یاور با همه خلق جهانیم
دوستدار جمله خلقیم و شر و غوغا نداریم	فرقه جوئی و ضلالت کی بود اندر خور ما
راد مردا بهتر از این جمله ای زیبا نداریم	هان که" لااکراه فی الدین" نص قرآن مبین است
ورنه جز عرفان با حق ملجاء و مأوی نداریم	ای دریغ افسوس بر تو سخت پابند هوائی
بهتر و محکم تر از این عروۀ الوثقی نداریم	پای بند دین و ایمان باش حقّانی که هرگز

۲۰

عبدی

سیمرغ عشق بر دل ما چون قدم نهاد	گنجشگ عقل سر به دیار عدم نهاد
در آینه چو کنز خفی خویشتن بدید	پرده گشود و صورت و معنی بهم نهاد
آیا چه دید گوهر پاک ذبیح عشق	کاین قصّه را به دفتر هستی رقم نهاد
آن کیست کز شهادت جانسوز خویشتن	آتش به جان مادر و اهل حرم نهاد
با سوز دل چو لاله خونین به پای سرو	سر را به پیش پای جمال قدم نهاد
آن غصن اطهرست که قبل از شهادتش	جان در سبیل شاهد لوح و قلم نهاد
دیدی که آتشی که وجود بدیع سوخت	داغ ابد به چهره شاه عجم نهاد
شیطان چو در مصاف حقیقت شکست خورد	قرآن گرفت و مُهر به پای قسم نهاد
ساقی به جام عیش تو عبدی ز مصلحت	یک جرعه هم ز بادهٔ شیرین غم نهاد

۲۱

عبدی

خمخانه عشق

نسیم گلشن آباده گر دل انگیزست	ز عطر شبنم گل‌های سرخ نی‌ریزست
در آن حدیقهٔ رحمان ز خون اهل وفاست	چو شعله، برگ شقایق اگر شررخیزست
نمانده غیر شهادت ز میکده راهی	نگاه مست تو ساقی چنین که خونریزست
بریز بادهٔ سرخ فنا به ساغر عشق	که جام صبر من از اشک دیده، لبریزست
مگر صبا سر کوی ترا زیارت کرد	که همچو نافهٔ مشک ختن دل‌آویزست
بهار ما تویی ای گل که بی تو در آفاق	طلوع صبح بهاران، غروب پاییزست
شها به چشم عنایت بر این گدا نظری	که مستحقّ نگاهی محبت آمیزست
از آن به کوی تو عبدی هنوز جان دارد	که جان نثار تو کردن حقیر و ناچیزست

۲۲

دیروز، امروز، فردا

گرمی پرسی که هستم امروز	هم فردای و هم السـتم امروز
من نیستم آن که دوش بـودم	فردا نیم آن که هستم امروز
کی پای بوقفه می‌توان بست	کز شوق سلوک مستم امروز
همواره کمال مقصد ماست	هرچند که خُرد و پستم امروز
از جبر زمان سخن مگوئید	کاین بند زجان گسستم امروز
چون مرغ فضای گلشن غیب	از بام زمانه جستم امروز
آرام و قرار از چه جـویم؟	کز هر چه درنگ رستم امروز
صیرورت و سیر قصّهٔ ماست	این راه بخود نبستم امروز
بس نکته هنوز در دلـم هست	دردا که قلم شکستم امروز

۲۳

محمد رضا حسامی

بنازم ساحت زیبای زندان	هوای دلکش دنیای زندان
خوشا ترتیل آیات و مناجات	سحرها گوشهٔ تنهای زندان
بیاد دوست بعد از حکم تعزیز	شدن سرمست از صهبای زندان
بیاد آوردن خیل شهیدان	همان پرپر شده گل‌های زندان
ز طوفان بلا در باغ و بستان	کجا شد مرغ خوش آوای زندان
بسا مجنون که اندر انفرادی	بسوزد در غم لیلای زندان
«شنیدن کی بود مانند دیدن»	مجسّم کی شود رؤیای زندان
قسم بر حضرت مسجون چهریق	علّی عالی اعلای زندان
به آن ذات قدیم سجن اعظم	جمال اقدس ابهای زندان
به غصن اعظم آن مولای عالم	که عمری بوده در عکّای زندان
به مولای توانا غصن ممتاز	ولّیی والی والای زندان
شود زندان گلستان بر حسامیّ	اگر راضی بود مولای زندان

۲٤

فخرالدین هوشنگ روحانی

همتی مردانه می‌خواهد زجان خود گسستن — محنت زندان کشیدن بر سر پیمان نشستن

شعله سرتا پا شدن، درعشق جانان جان سپردن — وز همه دلبستگی‌های جهان یکباره رستن

با محن الفت گرفتن در بلایا شاد بودن — دیدهٔ دل را بروی هرچه غیر از اوست بستن

۲۵

بهروز بهشتی

شب شکنان

آنانکه سر و جان ره جانان بفشانند	آزاد ز زندان زمانند و مکانند
از پرتو انوار بها غرقه به نورند	چون چهره خورشید سما نور فشانند
در راه بلا قافله سالار رضایند	در عشق و وفا آیت دوران و زمانند
کوبند ببازار فدا کوس شهادت	سودای دگر جز طلب یار ندانند
در اوج حقیقت پر اسرار گشایند	آسوده و دل کنده ز اوهام و گمانند
از ریزش رگبار جفا باک ندارند	چون بحر خروشنده کران تا به کرانند
از حملهٔ شب کور پر از کین نهراسند	در ظلمت یلدای بلا شب شکنانند
در عالم تن گرچه گرفتار و اسیرند	دیهیم به سر پادشه کشور جانند
در دشت فنا کشته و افتاده بخاکند	در ملک بقا زنده و جاوید بمانند

۲۶

صالح زاده سمرقندی

از گفتگوی خلق هراسان نمی‌شوم	سامانم اینکه بی سر و سامان نمی‌شوم
در پردلی چو شیرم و ترسان نمی‌شوم	زین بزدلان که سفسطه خوانند ژاژخای
من طفل نیستم به دبستان نمی‌شوم	خواندم بسی مطالب ایقان [و] درس عشق
البته چون تو بندهٔ احسان نمی‌شوم	من بنده‌ام به حق [و] حقیقی بهائیم،
بیهوده با تو دست و گریبان نمی‌شوم	گفتار من حدیث کلام حق است، از آن
حقا که هیچ باعث خسران نمی‌شوم	حقگوی و حق پذیرم و حقجوی و حقسرشت
در هیچ سینه باعث احزان نمی‌شوم	تا جان غمگزین به تنم جاگزین بود
از برق و باد حادثه لرزان نمی‌شوم	چون کوه ثابتم پی پیمان [و] عهد خویش
آماج تیر طعنه بهتان نمی‌شوم	صدق است گفته‌ام همه در نزد اهل دل
جمع است خاطرم که پریشان نمی‌شوم	گر صد هزار فتنه در آفاق رو دهد
نوحم که غرق لجه [و] طوفان نمی‌شوم	دنیا اگر بجوشش طوفان فرو شود

۲۷

عبدی

تا از دل و جان بندهٔ درگاه بهائیم	آزاد ز بند قفس نفس و هوائیم
درگلشن ایجاد چو مرغان بهاری	سرمست و سبکبال تر از باد صبائیم
آن جا که فروزنده بود شمع محبت	پروانهٔ دل سوختهٔ بزم وفائیم
هرگاه کند جور و جفا دشمن سفاک	جان بر کف و آماده به میدان فدائیم
ما ساکن میخانهٔ عشقیم و ازآن روی	دور از گذر کوچهٔ تزویر و ریائیم
در بحر پر امواج قضایای الهی	آسوده از آنیم که راضی به رضائیم
عبدی، تو گمان می‌کنی از فیض عبادت	بر عرش برین ساکن و محبوب خدائیم
حق را به دعای من و تو نیست نیازی	مائیم که محتاج مناجات و دعائیم

۲۸

فخرالدین هوشنگ روحانی

جام بلا

تـشنهٔ جـام بلایــم خـوف اهــریمن نــدارم سست عهدان بیم جان دارند اما من ندارم
گرکه از خویشم برانی یا که در ریشم بخوانی من بجز دامانت ای آرام جان مأمن ندارم
تا بـدل عـشق تـرا دارم ز کـس پـروا نـدارم تـا تـوئی یـار وفـا دارم غـم دشـمن نـدارم
ای خوشا رفـتن بـراه وصـل و دادن جان شرین پـای رفـتن دارم امـا همـت رفـتن نـدارم
در غـم نامردمیهـا و ز جورفتنــه کــاران جان بلـب دارم ولـیکن زاری و شیون نـدارم
تیـغ در دست رقیـب و حکـم از آن حسودان من بزیـر تیغ دشمن خـوف جان و تن ندارم
از بـلا دیگر مترسـان جـان درد آلـود مـارا من بـدل خوف عـدو را یـک سرسوزن نـدارم
ایـکه در حیرت شـدی از طاقـت و تـاب و توانم مـن بغیر از جامـه ایمـان بـتن جوشن نـدارم
مـوج تأییـد الهـی مـی‌رسـد بـر مـن دمـادم ورنه من خود طاقت این سیل بنیان کن ندارم
کامکـاران بـاد ارزانـی شـما را نقدهـستی من که جز خارستم سهمی در این گلشن ندارم
شعله بر جان بود و در بحر بلا می‌گفت ُسرکش تـشنهٔ جـام بلایــم خـوف اهــریمن نــدارم

۲۹

اوجی (شهید)

جانا برهت باختن جان مزه دارد / جان باختن اندر ره جانان مزه دارد
رسوا شدن و متّهم عشق تو بودن / بی جرم و گنه گوشه زندان مزه دارد
در گوشه زندان و ز دیدار عزیزان / گل چیدن و گل گفتن و خندان مزه دارد
لبخند ملیح از لب احباب گرفتن / وز کان نمک قند فراوان مزه دارد
اردنگی و فحّاشی و سیلی ندهد لطف / شلّاق جفا بر تن عریان مزه دارد
جمعیم بیاد سر زلف تو پریشان / آشفتگی جمع پریشان مزه دارد
نابت بگریز از بر افراد گران جان / بر روی زمین پیکر بی جان مزه دارد

۳۰

حسین قراچه داغی

جامه باقی

برافکن خلعت هستی ز تن گرمست جانانی	که لایق نیست عاشق را چنین پیراهن دانی
قبای سرخی از خون شهادت را تو در برکن	برآور جامه اوهام اگر از اهل عرفانی
بیا و خرقهٔ حق را بدوش خویش برگیرش	که شد برقامتت این خلعت تقدیس ارزانی
به بین تشریف توحیدی که شد بر هیکلت موزون	بدست آورده‌ای سختش مده آنرا بهآسانی
حریرش در فلک نبود، نظیرش نی به زردوزی	بود تارش ز عرفان، پودش از ایقان یزدانی
ز دست پیر دانائی برون آید چنین مصنوع	که خیاط توانایش ندارد در جهان ثانی
بود محصول آن مُلکی که سلطانش بود ابهی	نه حاجت بر رفو دارد نه بیند روی ویرانی
فزاید رونقش هردم نگردد جلوه‌هایش کم	طراوت‌ها نماید او به پیدائی و پنهانی
نیاید باوساخی رباید دیده‌ها را خوش	خوشا این جامهٔ باقی بر آن اندام روحانی

۳۱

سیروس روشنی (شهید)

تا سر به قدمگاه تو ای دوست گذارم	جان در ره امر تو چه آسان بسپارم
عمری است که در حسرت دیدار تو بگذشت	عمر دگری نیز چو اینک بسر آرم
جز صورت معشوق به آئینه دل نیست	جز گوهر یکدانه در این گنج ندارم
گر پروری از فضل و اگر بشکری از عدل	دلبسته به بند تو به دام تو شکارم
تا خدمت امر تو مرا فضل و کمال است	با زینت و با ثروت دنیاست چکارم؟
روی چو مهت آینهٔ طلعت روز است	موی سیهت خاطره‌ای از شب تارم
هرکس به امیدی پی مطلوب روان است	زاهد پی نقدینه و من طالب یارم
عنقای بقائی خبر از قاف وفا داد	و آن مژدهٔ جانانه ز دل برد قرارم
ابر سیه‌ام لیک ز نیسان نگارم	بارانم و یکسان به گُل و خار ببارم
بی خار میسّر نشود گل چو به بُستان	ای غنچهٔ نشگفته برمگیر که خارم
شهد سخنم بس مزه در ذائقه دارد	تا با شب شیرین تو افتد سر و کارم
زان بادهٔ خمّار حقیقت به خُم عشق	جامی بده ای ساقی باقی که خُمارم
مغبوط به ملک و ملکوتم چه مقامی؟!	سیروسم و بر کفش کن عشق غبارم

دامن کشان

همچو آتش در هوای دوست سر خواهم کشید	خرم آن روزی که دست از خشک و تر خواهم کشید
رخت از اینجا سوی دنیای سحر خواهم کشید	عالم ظلمت به خلق تیره دل خواهم نهاد
زین قفس زی گلشن جاوید پر خواهم کشید	چار دیوار تن فرسوده را خواهم شکست
لاجرم دامان از این دام خطر خواهم کشید	دانهٔ دنیا به کام طائر آزاده نیست
از رحیق عشق او جام شرر خواهم کشید	در حریم قدس حقّ دست طرب خواهم فشاند
نعرهٔ مستانهٔ دیدار بر خواهم کشید	پرده از رُخسارهٔ دلدار بر خواهم گرفت
خطّ بطلان بر همه زیر و زبر خواهم کشید	همچو پرگاری به گرد نقطهٔ خال نگار

۳۳

عبدی

قلب آتشین

گفتـا شهید عـشق، بـه مأمور قتـل خـویش   بعـد از ثنـا بـه درگــه محبـوُب عــالمین
کای رامی غیـور، بـدان کـاین گلوله نیست   کـز قهـر تـو بـسوی مـن آرد پیــام کـین
ایـن سـینه مـن اسـت کـه مردانـه مـی رود   سـوی گُلولـه‌هـای تـو بـا قلـب آتـشین

۳٤

فخرالدین هوشنگ روحانی

نام یک شهید

به کوچه‌های ستم تندباد فتنه وزید

و بر در و دیوار

غبار ظلم نشست

و بوی جهل و تعصب بهر طرف پیچید

و باز باردگر

کبوتری معصوم

بخون خود غلتید

و باز باردگر

نوای شادی گرگان ز رنگ خون برخاست

و روز سرخوشی و عیش و رقص شیطان شد.

دوباره ظلمت ظلم

براه نور نشست

و دست هرزه بیداد نوگلی را چید

و شاخه‌ای بشکست.

چه پاک بود کبوتر

که رفت تا به بهشت

چه خوب بود بهشت

که باز بر در خود نام یک شهید نوشت

۳۵

منوچهر حجازی

جان رقص کنان سوی جنان شد شده باشد / تن بر سر بازار کشان شد شده باشد

در مسلک عاشق خبر از عقل چه گیرید / دل باخته بی‌نام و نشان شد شده باشد

طوفان حوادث نکند ریشهٔ شوقت / برگت اگرش برگ وزان شد شده باشد

جان معرض تحقیر نگردد که چه حیف است / تن طعمهٔ مقراض کسان شد شده باشد

زیر پی ارکان ادب آب نیفتد / سیلاب به کاشانه روان شد شده باشد

حُرّیّت ایمان ترا از تو نگیرند / زنجیر اسارت به میان شد شده باشد

من این غزل نغز به پیش تو فرستم / همراه غزل هدیه جان شد شده باشد

۳۶

فخرالدین هوشنگ روحانی

خوب جاودانه

ای خوب جاودانه که پرواز کرده‌ای
تا عرش کبریا،
ای خوب جاودانه که رفتی به اوج‌ها
برممکن وفا،
ای همطراز صدرنشینان بارگاه
ای همنشین جمله خوبان پاکباز
ای فاتح بلندترین قله‌های عشق
ای رفته تا فراز،
ای خوب جاودانه که ایثار و بندگی
در قلب پر عطوفت تو شکل می‌گرفت
ای خوب تر زخوب
باور نکرده‌ایم،
باور نکرده‌ایم که از ما بریده‌ای
ای خوب جاودانه که رفتی و برده‌ای
از قلب ما توان و شکیب و قرار را
با چشمهای دوخته بر راههای دور
تا واپسین عمر
بر دوش می‌کشیم غم انتظار را،

وصال یار

از همسرت اگر چه جدا گشته‌ای ولیک
روح شما یکیست
آنسان که قلبتان
در گوش او همیشه نواهای گرم تست
او با خیال خاطره‌های تو زنده است
او خوانده بود قصهٔ تلخ فراق‌ها
اما نداشت طاقت این درد و داغ‌ها
او می‌شنید از غم از هم بریده‌ها
اما ندیده بود چنین غم به دیده‌ها
او صحبت پیام تراگوش می‌کند
یعنی صفای قلب ترا نوش می‌کند
او با دلی شکسته و با چشم اشکبار
بس شکوه‌ها که با لب خاموش می‌کند
فرزند مهربان تو امید قلب ماست
او خاطرات خوب ترا زنده می‌کند
او باده می‌شود که بریزد به جام‌ها
او شهد می‌شود که بتابد به شام‌ها
او صحبت از محبت پاینده می‌کند
او خاطرات خوب ترا زنده می‌کند
زیرا پیام عشق ترا آورد بیاد
او هم عطای دیگری از رحمت خداست
او روی و موی و خوی ترا آورد بیاد

وصال یار

آری هر آنچه بوی ترا میدهد نکوست
فرزند خردسال تو تا سالهای سال
یاد ترا بخاطره‌ها زنده می‌کند
او صحبت از محبت پاینده می‌کند
هرگز گمان مبر که تو از یاد می‌روی
یاد تو زنده است و نام تو نیز هم

۳۷

شاپور مرکزی (شهید)

نمی‌دانم چرا دل بی‌قرار است   طپشهایش شدید و بی‌شمار است
وجودم را دوباره کرده تسخیر   غمی کانرا نه حد و نه مدار است

دوباره سیف عصیان گشته کاری   بریده رشته امیدواری
چنان مایوس و محزون و غمینم   که روحم شد زهر تابنده عاری

مرا دیروز هر دم چشم تر بود   که آن چشم ترم هم سوی در بود
مصور بر دلم نقش عزیزان   مجلّی چهره دخت و پسر بود

امیدم عاقبت نیکو ثمر داد   نگهبانم به دیداری خبر داد
در آغوشم فشردم قلب و روحم   خبر این لحظه از درد دگر داد

وداعی گرم و جانسوز و غمین بود   هزاران غم مرا از پی کمین بود
برفت از دیده‌ام نور و ز دل روح   تمام روح و جانم هر دو این بود

وصال یار

دگر امید دیداری ندارم که جز حرمان و غم‌کاری ندارم
توکل کن دلا بر لطف جانان دعا کن تا شود بیرون ز تن جان
فدای حضرت محبوب گردی نگردی همنشین با رنج و حرمان

عزیزانت بحقّ بسپار و برگرد قدم در راه مردی نه توای مرد
دگر فکر عزیزانت رها کن که گردی تورها از غصه و درد

۳۸

اوجی (شهید)

وای بر من اگر امضای قدر دیر شود	ای خوش آن لحظه که قلبم هدف تیر شود
که از او سلطنت عشق جهانگیر شود	دم عشاق جگر سوخته را تأثیری ست
هر زمان دامن جان گیرد و درگیر شود	گیروداری ست در این راه خطرناک که دل
چون گرفتار غم هجر شود پیر شود	پیر را عشق جوان سازد و هر تازه جوان
عاشق از سوز تب عشق ز جان سیر شود	تشنگان در طلب آب روانند ولی
یار با ما سر صلح آید و تعبیر شود	دیده‌ام خوابی و امید که در اسرع وقت
هان مبادا که در این مرحله تأخیر شود	کرده محکوم با عدام مرا حاکم شرع
جای دارد که در این جامعه تکفیر شود	نابتاً ار بانک اناالحق بزند چون منصور

۳۹

عبدی

بیاد شید رُخ

رؤیای دختری در شهادت مادرش

مادر مرا ببخش که روز شهادتت	برگ گلی ز اشک نثارت نکرده‌ام
مادر مرا ببخش کزین اشک جانگداز	یک قطره هم نثار مزارت نکرده‌ام
مادر بگو که قلب وفا پرور ترا	تیر جفای خلق، چگونه هدف گرفت
با آنکه در ثبوت محبّت به نقد عشق	آن جان پاک، گوهر جان را به کف گرفت
ای رامی گلولهٔ رگبار آتشین	بگذر ز قهر خویش که بیداد می‌کنی
اکنون که میکُشی تو به فتوای ظالمین	از چه ستم به مدفن اجساد می‌کنی
ای قبله‌گاه عالم هستی نگاه کن	خلق جهان به کینه و نفرت چه می‌کنند
ما طالب وفا و ببین خلق روزگار	در پاسخ ندای محبّت چه می‌کنند
آه ای گلوله‌های جگرسوز بگذرید	از خون این عزیز که این مادر من است
این نازنین کبوتر معصوم و بی‌گناه	تنها نه مادرست که تاج سرم من است
این دختر شهید چنین گفت و اشک ریخت	اشکی که دُرّ به دامن مهتاب سُفته بود
وقتی که ماه و زهره به خواب گران شدند	آن دیدگان خسته و بیمار خفته بود
رفت از جهان خاک و فراتر زآسمان	فرزند نیک بخت به رُؤیای مادرش
پاکیزه‌تر ز آینه در هاله‌ای ز نور	دید عاشقانه، صورت زیبای مادرش
بگشود آن پری لب خندان خویش را	چون غنچهٔ بهار، به گلبوسهٔ نسیم

کای دختر عزیز من ای نوردیده‌ام   ای قطره‌های اشک تو چون چشمه نعیم
کردی گمان که تیر جفاکار ظالمین   روح مرا ز محبس عالم رها نمود
غافل که جان تشنهٔ من در وصال دوست   خود آرزوی مشهد قدس فدا نمود
بودم غمین و خسته به زندان مرگبار   جان در تب عذاب و اسیر شکنجه بود
رویم کبود گشته ز سیلی و همچنان   پشتم ز داغ و ضربه شلّاق رنجه بود
تا آنکه در سرادق افلاکیان قدس   آسود جان خسته و اندوه بار من
امضاء نمود کلک قضا لوح احمرم   پایان گرفت رنج من و انتظار من
اکنون ببین که به بهر ثنایم فرشتگان   صف بسته تا سریر شه مکمن بقا
با نغمه ملائکه فوج طیور عرش   خواند سرود تهنیت و مژدهٔ لقا
اکنون زغرفه‌ای که بود از حریر نور   در جلوه‌هاست شاهد اقبال و آرزو
گوید که ای شهید فلک جاه و سربلند   اینک بگو به اهل زمین و زمان بگو
فرخنده باد طالع نسوان که از رجال   سبقت گرفت و گوی محبت به جان ربود
بنگر هُمای بخت زنان را که بسته بود   در آسمان امر چسان بال و پر گشود
آری تو از تبار شهیدی ولی بدان   میراث من برای تو تنها نه این بود
آنجا که جایگاه رفیع ملائک است   گلبانگ سی هزار شهیدان چنین بود
هر چند افتخار شهادت به لطف دوست   فرخنده خلعتی است که تاج سعادتست
لیکن قیام و خدمت امرش به شرط صدق   بالاتر از مقام بلند شهادتست

٤٠

عبدی

شاهد قدسم اگر باز زجا برخیزد	نعرهٔ عشق ز خاک شهداء برخیزد
گر نسیمی وزد از موی پریشان نگار	باز هم عطر گل از باد صبا برخیزد
گیرد از اشک روان دامن آن سروبلند	عاشقی گر نتواند که به پا برخیزد
حاسدار مهر جهانتاب به زنجیر کشد	باز از کنج سیه چال ندا برخیزد
سر عاشق سپر سینهٔ محبوب شود	اگر از حادثه صد تیر بلا برخیزد
بخت محمود نژاد است که از لالهٔ رخان	بین عشّاق یکی همچو مُنا برخیزد
سوخت پروانه و می‌گفت که در پرتو عشق	نالهٔ شوق ز خاکستر ما برخیزد
عبدی از خصم مکن شکوه که گلبانگ فلاح	از دم خون شهیدان بها برخیزد

۴۱

عزیز حکیمیان

شهید

در سکوت لحظه‌ها، در دل اندیشه‌ها
از صدای تیشه فرهادها
در دیار بادها
بر فراز چوب‌دار
در گل و گلزار و باغ و لاله‌زار
از دل عشاق از غم بیقرار
در میان خون و خاک
در میان اشک تاک
از سیاهی شب و صبح سپید
هست رمزی از پیامت ای شهید

۴۲

عبدی

آزاده

آن عاشقی که حسرت جان را نداشته است	غیر از وصال دوست، تمنّا نداشته است
دلدادهٔ شهید، در ایثار خون خویش	باکی ز قهر و کینهٔ اعدا نداشته است
باران رعدخیز، به طوفان حادثات	ترسی ز موج و دهشت دریا نداشته است
طیر بقا به عرضهٔ افلاک، مقصدی	جز آشیان باقی عنقا نداشته است
خرّم دلی که تشنه به روز شهادتش	غیر از شراب عشق، به مینا نداشته است
گلبانگ یا بهای شهیدان چو این زمان	در شرق و غرب اینهمه غوغا نداشته است
هرگز عقاب تیز، به رگبار آتشین	مرگی چنین صمیمی و زیبا نداشته است
گلگشت نوبهار، چنین لاله‌های سرخ	هنگام گل به دامن صحرا نداشته است
این غنچه‌های گل که در ایران شکفته‌اند	باغ ارم به جنّت عُلیا نداشته است
دنیا اگر سرای غم است و مکان زاغ	شهباز عشق، خود غم دنیا نداشته است
آری نداشته است بهائی جهان خاک	آزاده آنکه حبّ جهان را نداشته است

٤٣

عبدی

دور از رُخ تو گر شب ما را سحری نیست		جز روی توام پرتو صبح دگری نیست
گر نیست مرا خلوت پروانهٔ عشقی		آن شمع خموشم که به آهم شرری نیست
باشد که شوم مشت غباری به کف باد		جز این به سرکوی تو ما را گذری نیست
آن مرغ اسیرم که مرا در غم جانان		آوای دلی هست اگر بال و پری نیست
ای وای که در غربتم از موطن معشوق		غیر از خبر مرگ عزیزان خبری نیست
فریاد که اجساد شهیدان بهائی		پامال چنان شد که از ایشان اثری نیست
نخل از ثمر خویش خورد سنگ حوادث		آسوده بود خار که او را ثمری نیست
عبدی دل پر نخوت و خالی ز محبت		ماند صدفی را که درونش گهری نیست

٤٤

عبدی

ای بسا ذلت که روزی دولت جاوید گشت   صُبح عالمتاب را ما در شب غم دیده‌ایم

مائیم همان مُرغ اسیری که کُشندش   در شام عزاداری و در جشن عروسی

نیست ما را بیمی از گرداب امواج بلا   مُرغ دریا دل کجا اندیشه از طوفان کند

ایّوب را نبوده چنین صبر و طاقتی   ما را چنانکه زحمت و آزار می‌دهند

٤٥

عبدی

چه میخواهد

نمیدانم که خلق از جان ما دیگر چه می‌خواهد — از این جمع اسیران بلا دیگر چه می‌خواهد
از این مشت ضعیفان پریشان‌حال و سرگردان — که هستی داده بر باد فنا دیگر چه می‌خواهد
صد و سی سال کُشت و سوخت اجساد شهیدان را — نمی‌دانم که از اهل بها دیگر چه می‌خواهد
خدا را ظالمی از ظالم دیگر نمی‌پرسد — کز این آوارگان بهر خدا دیگر چه می‌خواهد
از آن طفل یتیم نازپرورد و دل آزرده — که از دامان مادر شد جدا دیگر چه می‌خواهد
از آن پیر علیل و داغدار از قتل فرزندش — که شد کاشانه‌اش ماتم‌سرا دیگر چه می‌خواهد
اگر شد از عداوت شوهری محکوم و زندانی — ز طفل و همسر آن بینوا دیگر چه می‌خواهد
نمی‌پرسد چرا آزاده‌ای از اهل ظلم آخر — چه می‌خواهد چه می‌خواهد ز ما دیگر چه می‌خواهد

٤٦

فرهمند مقبلین

ای دل افسرده از نو شاد شو	ترک کن ویرانه را آباد شو
ای پرستوی غمین و خسته جان	پَرزن از کنج قفس آزاد شو
تا به کی بر لب زنی مهر سکوت	بشکن این خاموشی و فریاد شو
شام تار غم به پایان آمده	ای سیه روای ستم بر باد شو
می‌رسد از دوست پیغامی دگر	ای بهشت آرزو بنیاد شو
زنگ هر افسردگی از جان بشوی	شادی هر بندهٔ ناشاد شو
خون گُلگون شهیدان کذب نیست	پُرنوا شو موج شو بی‌داد شو
نقش خاطر شو تو ای امر بزرگ	وی تو هر تردید رو از یاد شو
فرصتی دیگر تو را اُلهامٌ نیست	موجب دلشادی اجداد شو

٤٧

چیست این فردوس بر کوه خدا	پله پله تا به عرش کبریا؟
بوستانی در هوا آویخته	سنگ‌ها با رنگ‌ها آمیخته
بس چمن با گل هم آغوش آمده	چشمه و فواره در جوش آمده
از بنفشه تپه‌ها رنگین شده	بوته‌ها با تاج گل تزیین شده
سروهای ناز صف بسته ردیف	وز نسیم صبح در موج لطیف
باد چون بر باغ بالا بگذرد	عطری از نارنج شیراز آورد
بیتُ سلطان رسل آید به یاد	وان درخت خرم نیکو نهاد
گر که دشمن آن شجر از ریشه کند	بذر او را حق به هر بومی فکند
در میان کوه صد گونه شجر	سرکشیده از دل خاک و حجر
هر یکی شاداب‌تر از دیگری	در نظر چون بیرق هر کشوری
کوه کرمل گشته زین رو سر به سر	خیمهٔ یکرنگیِ نوع بشر
طرفه معجونی است این باغ عجیب	کز فراز کوه آید تا نشیب
سرخ و سبز و آبی و زرد و بنفش	هرچه دل خواهد در او از رنگ و نقش
از گل و از سبزه پل‌ها بسته‌اند	آسمان را با زمین پیوسته‌اند
جلوه‌گاه هرچه حسن سرمدی است	آیتی از باغ‌های ایزدی است
بنگر آن پیکر تراش چیره دست	این همه باز از کجا آورده است؟
بازهایی تیز چشم و تیز بال	شاهد آن صحنه مجد و جلال
مرغ‌ها از هر کران گرد آمده	شادمان در نغمه و ورد آمده
جمله گویی در مناجات و نماز	از نداشان کوه و در در اهتزاز
بیمی اینجا از عقاب سنگ نیست	طائری با طائری در جنگ نیست

وصال یار

شب چو آید با ردای قیرگون	روشنی از روز هم گردد فزون
کوه کرمل را چراغانی کنند	کهکشان مانند نورانی کنند
خاطرات قلعهٔ ماکو از آن	زنده گردد در دل بینندگان
وان سکوت و ظلمت و حبس شدید	که جهان چون وی نه دید و نه شنید
اشک‌ها از دیده ریزد بی قیاس	پرتو کرمل در او در انعکاس

٤٨

ابهی

ای بهـاءالله، جـان قربـان تـو   چـون بـود نـور خـدا در جـان تـو
تـا تـو از ایـران زمین برخاستی   شـوکت و فـرش بـود از شأن تـو
کـاش میدیـدی کـه این نابخردان   خـود چـه هـا کردنـد بـا ایران تـو
چـون تـو فرمـان خدا را می بـری   می پـذیرد هـر کسـی فرمـان تـو
کـار تـو از بـسکه حیـرت زا بـود   می شـود هـر شاهدی حیران تـو
دردمنـد دیـن اگـر باشـد کـسی   چـارۀ او نیـست جـز درمان تـو
مـن بهـائی نیـستم امـا بجـان   می شناسـم ارزش ایمـان تـو
تـا رهـا گـردیم از هـر آفتـی   دسـت مـا و گوشـه دامـان تـو

۴۹

اقدس توفیقی

سلام ای سرزمین شادی و غم	سلام ای موطن محبوب عالم
گرامی ملت با فرّ یزدان	سلام ای زادگاه شیرمردان
که ظاهر شد ز تو گنجینهٔ راز	سلام ای شهر شورانگیز شیراز
به آن زیبائی نصف جهانت	سلام من به شهر اصفهانت
فداکاری کسی این سان ندیده	دو جسم پاک در آن آرمیده
ولکن روحشان باشد در افلاک	بخفتند آن هیاکل در دل خاک
ز خون رب اعلی گشته گلریز	سلام من به خاک پاک تبریز
به آن قربانیان خاک کویت	سلام آرم به یزد با شکوهت
به روح پر فتوح آن شهیدان	سلام من به یک یک شهر ایران
هزاران سینهٔ مشتاق بی کین	به طهرانت هزاران جان شیرین
مُشبک شد ز تیر جور اعداء	که بُد مملو ز مهر و عشق ابهی
به آن نیکو جوانان امینت	سلام من به جمع مؤمنینت
به راه عشق آن مقصود امکان	نموده جان شیرین را به قربان
سزد گر سرزمینت گردد آباد	تو فخر عالم و عالم به تو شاد

۵۰

هوشمند فتح‌اعظم

وصال یار

دامـن کـشـان برفــت و کـسـی را نــشـان نـبـود	چـون بـاد خـوش وزیـد و بجـا یکزمـان نبـود
بـا بـرق یـک نگـه کـه بعـالم روانـه سـاخت	زد آتـشی چنـان کـه دلـی در امـان نبـود
رفتم بپـای شـوق کـه جـان در رهـش دهم	جـانم نثـار بـود ولـی جـان سـتـان نبـود
بــرگلبن امیــد چــه بیجـا گریـــسـتم	اشـگ روان چـه سـود کـه سـروروان نبـود
گفتـم مگـر کـه دامـن تـو آیـدم بدسـت	گفتـا بـرو بـرو کـه تـرا آن تـوان نبـود
مـور غریـق، راه ز دریـا بـرون نبـرد	مــرغ جــریـح طـایـر آن آشـیـان نبـود
شـرط لیاقـت اسـت و طلـب قـرب دوسـت را	از بخـت شـور ماسـت کـه این بـود و آن نبـود
جـز ذره غبـار کـه بـر دامـنش نشـست	راهـی دگـر ز بهـر وصـالش عیـان نبـود
پـس خـاک راه بـاش تـو و برتـو بگـذرد	آن یـار بی نشـان کـه چـو ا و در جهـان نبـود
ایـدل بـشارتت کـه حـصول وصـال یـار	دور از کــرم نمــائی آن مهربـان نبـود